The
Beautiful Blonde
Library Angel

The Beautiful Blonde Library Angel

Phillip Parcheminer

Library of Congress Control Number:		2019942657
ISBN:	Hardcover	978-1-7960-3385-4
	Softcover	978-1-7960-3384-7
	eBook	978-1-7960-3383-0

Rev. date: 11/20/2020

To order additional copies of this book, contact:
Xlibris
844-714-8691
www.Xlibris.com
Orders@Xlibris.com
794968

Contents

The Beautiful Blonde Library Angel

I was spending another day at the library obsessing over my beautiful blonde library angel. I was spending most of my days at the library obsessing over her. The more time that I spent at the library obsessing over her, the more my obsession with this beautiful angel grew. The more my obsession with her grew, the more she was inspiring me to follow my spiritual journey with her by providing me with the hope of someday meeting a beautiful woman like her.

The most spiritual of all my days spent at the library obsessing over her had to be Saturdays because Saturdays were my Latin days. I am not sure when exactly Saturdays started to be my Latin days. However, I had always associated Saturdays with all things Latin. So, Saturdays were my days for listening to Spanish music and for eating Spanish food. It was my love for Spanish music though, that made Saturdays such inspirational days at the library. Another reason why Saturdays were so inspirational had to be because this was a day she was usually working. So, throughout my spiritual journey of obsessing over her, I found I was starting to think of these Saturdays as being my most spiritual and inspirational day at the library.

I started spending most of my Saturdays at the library listening to Spanish music and obsessing over my beautiful blonde library angel. I even started associating a Spanish song with my obsession with her because of these Saturdays. This Spanish song was "Vuela Libre Paloma" or "Fly Free, My Dove" when translated into English. This song was about someone's guardian angel leading them out of the darkness of their reality. Once I translated the lyrics to this song, I realized it was all about my spiritual journey with my beautiful blonde library angel. After discovering this song, I started feeling her spiritual presence every time I heard it play. This beautiful blonde library angel was starting to turn into my beacon of hope at a time when I lost all hope. This beacon of hope was all I had to look forward to once I fell into my pit of darkness. Gradually, my beautiful blonde librarian turned into my beautiful blonde library angel.

The story of my spiritual journey with the beautiful blonde library angel starts with me going to the library to get a glimpse of her whenever I got the chance. I never could get enough of seeing my beautiful blonde library angel at the library. It could be the darkest of days, then once I got a glimpse of her beauty my darkness started to fade away. These glimpses of her beauty were also leading me out of my pit of darkness. Eventually, these glimpses were even inspiring me to start a new path for my life. Thus, I started spending hour after hour, day after day at the library trying to catch a glimpse of my beautiful blonde library angel. The more time I spent at the library obsessing over her, the more she turned into my source of inspiration. So, as I start to write about my spiritual journey with her, I must warn you that this is not a love story. This story is not of a man who got the woman of his dreams. Instead, this story is about the spiritual journey that I took once I got my very first glimpse of my beautiful blonde library angel.

My story is about all of the changes that I went through after I started my spiritual journey with her. The first of these changes was with how I viewed my obsession with her. At the start of my spiritual journey, I was ashamed and embarrassed by my obsession with her. I was feeling all this shame and embarrassment because of my social anxiety. Then, I made a powerful choice to ignore my feelings and follow my obsession with her wherever it might lead.

Nothing was going to stop me from seeing where my obsession with her might lead. I was not going to let work stop me from seeing where this obsession with her might lead. I was not going to let what others might be thinking keep me from seeing where it might lead. I was not going to let what I thought she was thinking keep me from seeing where it might lead. Finally, I was not going to let my inability to socialize keep me from seeing where it might lead.

My inability to socialize was the main reason why I was never able to go beyond my obsession with the beautiful blonde library angel. I knew that I was never going to be able to say anything to her. Today, I am grateful that I never spoke to her though since this allowed me to always see her as this beautiful, perfect angel. I believe that speaking to her might have shattered this illusion that I had of her. This illusion was important because it gave me my hope.

Hope was a powerful thing during my spiritual journey because it was this hope that was going to help me find my way out of my pit of darkness. It was going to lead me out of my pit of darkness by introducing me to my passion for writing. My passion for writing was leading me out of my pit of darkness by giving me a way to communicate with the rest of the world. I knew I could not verbally communicate with people, so I hoped to communicate through my writing. The more I started to cultivate my passion for writing, the more I felt my confidence start to increase. Thus, I found that my passion for writing was starting to turn into a source of strength.

Hope was also what gave me the confidence to start running seven days a week. I was running seven days a week to be more physically attractive to beautiful women. It was my belief that I needed to be more physically attractive since I was already living at a disadvantage. This disadvantage was that I was living with social anxiety. This social anxiety had me believing that I was never going to be able to be the initiator of a conversation with a beautiful woman. I knew that I could not make the first move and approach a beautiful woman to ask her out. So, I believed that the only way I might ever have a chance with her was if I could be more attractive.

Hope was also the reason why I started looking into going back to work. I knew the importance of making money and that going back to work was my only way of making money. Now, the problem with me having to go back to work to make money was that I never really valued money. I felt time was more something I valued since it helped me develop my writing.

My passion for writing was what gave me the greatest joy. This made time my most valuable resource. Yet, I knew money was the most valuable resource for the rest of the world. I knew I needed to make money to pay my parents. I knew I needed to make money to attract a beautiful woman because this was the way of the world. I did not believe a beautiful woman could ever be attracted to a man without money or looks. Thus, I felt I had no choice other than to accept the fact that I was going to need both money and looks to attain a beautiful woman. Sadly, I had neither one of these things at the start of my spiritual journey with this library angel.

I was also lacking the confidence to approach beautiful women. I did not realize the importance of having confidence until I started my spiritual journey. At the start of my spiritual journey, I had no confidence to approach beautiful women. Then, I discovered my passion for writing, and I felt my confidence start to build internally. Once I was able to build my confidence, I blocked out my inadequacies enough to think I had a chance with beautiful women.

I started to realize I was gaining confidence with my passion for writing while I was obsessing over my beautiful blonde library angel. This was the power of my beautiful blonde library angel. Once I got a glimpse of her beauty, all of my fears and anxiety about my obsessions with her disappeared. It was because of this power that I thought of her as my beautiful blonde library angel. I started to think of her as this angel because there was so much more to her than mere beauty, although she was very beautiful. However, there were other angels to match her beauty during my spiritual journey with her. Yet, none of these angels ever matched her spiritual energy. They never matched her spiritual energy because of when she arrived into my life. She arrived into my life at a time when I needed someone or something to lead me out of my pit of darkness. Another reason why her spiritual energy could never be surpassed was that she never left the library until I wrote all about my spiritual journey with her. Her beauty and timing created a spiritual energy that was timeless. It was going to be this spiritual energy that I was feeling from her that turned her into my beautiful blonde library angel.

My beautiful blonde library angel was going to be my first of many guiding lights. My beautiful blonde library angel helped me find the confidence to follow my own path. So, I knew I was not leaving the library if she was still present since she gave birth to my spiritual journey. I was never going to leave her physical presence since she was guiding me to a better future. She was guiding me toward a future as a writer. My passion for writing was instilling me with the confidence to run, get back to work, live my life by my own rules, and also to be a better person.

It saddens me to know that this beautiful blonde library angel will never know the tremendous amount of power she had over me at the library. It saddens me to know that she will never know how much she inspired my life by giving birth to my spiritual journey with her. I know the true power of her beauty though and this is what really counts. So, I knew there were only going to be two reasons why I was going leave the library. One reason was if she quit. The other reason was if I found success as a writer. My definition of success was different from other people's definition because I never did not define success as making a great deal of money. I did not believe money was going to make me successful because money was not something I truly valued. Money was something the rest of the world valued to define success. I understood the importance of money if you wanted to buy certain things and to survive. However, beyond that, I did not see the value of making that much money. I did not value money like other people because I did not have a family to support. Yet, I knew how much the rest of the world valued money. Thus, my spiritual journey with my beautiful blonde library angel started with me writing about my personal struggle with how the world valued money and how I valued my time.

The inspiration I felt from seeing my beautiful blonde library angel never faltered. I always felt an energy flow through me the moment I got a glimpse of her. Thus, the day when I had to say goodbye to her was going to be a very sad and depressing day. It was going to be a day that I was going to dread. However, I also knew this was a day that I could survive. I believed that this was a day that I could survive because of all the valuable lessons that I learned.

One valuable lesson I learned was that my passion for writing had the power to heal. I discovered its power to heal after suffering two devastating losses. The first of these losses was when I was rejected by another library angel. Her rejection introduced me to the power my passion for writing had to heal by giving me an outlet for the pain and devastation I was feeling. The other devastating loss that led me to finding its power to heal was going to be the death of my father. The death of my father was truly devastating. However, my passion for writing gave me an outlet for this grief that I was feeling. I knew I could not verbally express this grief that I was feeling to anyone because of my social anxiety. Thus, I wrote my way through the grief. Then, this same passion for writing was how I also dealt with her supposed loss from the library.

I knew my spiritual journey with her never developed into a romantic relationship. I never even spoke to her other than the one time I thanked her for being so beautiful. However, this relationship was still one of the greatest relationships I remembered ever having. This relationship was going to last me about two-and-a-half years. My spiritual journey with her was going to teach me a great deal about myself. Thus, it was still going to be a very difficult loss to get over whenever it finally happened. However, it was going to be a loss I knew I could get over because I had gotten over her supposed loss before. I say supposed because she was only gone for two weeks when she returned to the library for a year. During her supposed loss, I discovered my passion for music. Also, this supposed loss led me to the story of my first book.

The story of the first book I was hoping to publish was going to be about my spiritual journey with the beautiful blonde library angel. It was going to be about how my obsession with her led me to my passion for writing. This was a two-and-a-half-year journey that I could never verbalize with words because of my debilitating social anxiety. Thus, the only way I knew how to tell my story was going to be through the writing of this book. This was a story that I felt needed to be told because it was a story about a man who was living with social anxiety. However, this story was going to be seen from a different perspective than many of the other books out there about social anxiety. My story was not about a man who confronted and defeated his social anxiety. Instead, it was about a man who learned to accept his social anxiety.

I never thought that I was going to be able to escape my debilitating social anxiety. I thought I had to learn to accept the jealousy I felt from watching everyone socialize so naturally. When I saw others socializing, I was only able to look at them with awe since socializing brought me so much discomfort. However, this acceptance did not mean that I had lost all hope of ever trying to change. I still hoped to find a way of gaining the confidence to socialize with people one day. At least, I was still hoping to find a way to talk to a beautiful woman someday because this was all that really mattered. After all, nobody really wants to live a life completely isolated and alone, myself included. Yet, I realized that as much strength as I got from my world of isolation and my passion for writing, there was only one way for me to ever be with someone. I knew that the only way I was ever going to meet someone was if I made some effort to socialize with people, especially with a beautiful woman. I believed I had to think outside the box to find a way to socialize with people. I knew that I was never going to be able to be the initiator of a conversation with a beautiful woman, or anyone for that matter. I turned to my passion for writing as way for me to communicate because of the severity of my social anxiety.

My journey of communicating with the world started with discovering the beautiful blonde library angel. This discovery led me to the introduction of my passion for writing. Once I discovered my passion for writing, I felt as if I had been reawakened from a dark slumber which had lasted my entire existence. I felt as if I had spent my entire life lost and confused without having any direction. Once I was reawakened, though, all of this changed and there was no way I was ever going back to my old life of being lost and confused. I knew that my passion for writing was the reason for me being put upon this earth. I also knew that it was going to be the only way that I was ever going to find the strength and confidence to start living a better life. I did not know how this was going to happen. I only knew that this was the only way I would be able to find any success of achieving the changes I needed to make to get a beautiful woman. I knew there was a chance my spiritual journey might never lead me to the woman of my dreams. However, this spiritual journey was the only path I knew how to follow due to my social anxiety. Therefore, it was my belief that I had to stay true to this path, ignoring what the rest of the world might think or say about this being the wrong path. I believed that the path of my spiritual journey with the beautiful blonde library angel was the right path and this was all that mattered.

The path of my spiritual journey with her was not a clear path. However, it was a path that I started living every day of my life and it was a path I was paving through my passion for writing.

This book was only the first book of a series of books that I was planning to write and present to the world. This was a series of books that I feared might never see the light of day at the start of my spiritual journey with her since I was not sure if they might ever get published. However, I guess if you are reading them, then I did get them published. This series of books could have never been possible had I not taken a chance and followed my own path. Once I started following my own path, I finally started my spiritual journey with my passion for writing.

This journey of hope with my passion for writing was going to start the moment I discovered the beauty of my beautiful blonde library angel. This beautiful blonde library angel was going to turn into more than a beautiful woman that I obsessed over. There were many beautiful women I had been obsessed over during my life's journey and each one felt special. However, none of them matched the spiritual energy of this beautiful blonde library angel because she arrived into my life at a time when I fell into a pit of darkness. I fell into this pit of darkness because I lost my future as a truck driver. So, again, I am not trying to take anything away from these beautiful women. They simply were not the beautiful blonde library angel. They were simply beautiful women that I was obsessed over and imagined having a family with one day. Whereas my obsession with this beautiful blonde library angel, went beyond this imagined life of one day being able to socialize with her and possibly having a family with her.

I was imagining having a life with her at the start of my spiritual journey. I knew that this was never going to happen though because of my social anxiety. However, this did not stop me from going to the library to see her beauty whenever I got the chance. My obsession with her beauty and the loss of truck driving gave birth to my spiritual journey with her. The loss of my future as a truck driver led me into my pit of darkness. My fall into this pit of darkness had me letting go of this imagined life with her since I knew she was out of my league. I knew that she was out of my league because I was twice her age. She was only about twenty years old and I was forty-one-years old. Also, I knew she had a boyfriend because I saw him at the library romancing her all summer. Then, I saw her with an engagement ring, and I knew that she was unavailable. Another reason why I thought she was out of my league was because she was so socially outgoing. Finally, my social anxiety was the real reason why I thought she was unattainable. My debilitating social anxiety had me thinking I could not talk to her or any other beautiful woman. It had me believing that I could not talk to anyone. I believed that my inability to socialize was my life's handicap. Then, I was introduced to my passion for writing.

My beautiful blonde library angel introduced me to my passion for writing. She also reawakened my passion for music. My passion for music and my passion for writing led to the creation of my world of isolation. Once my world of isolation was created, I found a place where I was going to be able to cultivate my writing for hours at a time, day after day. I never felt safer or more alive than when I entered my world of isolation. This world of isolation was where my spiritual journey with my beautiful blonde library angel was going to unfold. The more time that I spent within my world of isolation, the more I wrote about this spiritual journey. However, it was not until after I was done mourning over her supposed loss from the library that I was going to realize that my spiritual journey with her was going to be the story of my first book. So, I believe her supposed loss was as important as my discovery of her at the library. Luckily, she returned from this supposed loss though to inspire me as I wrote about this journey.

I spent four years creating the story of my spiritual journey with my beautiful blonde library angel. I spent the first two years of my spiritual journey with her being obsessed over her at the library. During these two years, I was introduced to my passion for writing that then started my spiritual journey with her. Then, once I thought she left the library for good, I started writing the story of my spiritual journey with her. It took me about seven months to create the story of my spiritual journey with her. I finally finished writing the story of my spiritual journey with her during Christmas 2017. Then, I spent most of 2018 getting my first book published. Sadly, I only sold nine copies of my first book after getting my first book published which was very disappointing. So, I read my book to see why it was not selling. Then, I created this updated version of *The Beautiful Blonde Library Angel* which starts with me introducing myself.

A Man Without A Voice

I was and I still am a man without a voice. There was no physical reason why I was a man without a voice. I did not have a medical condition that caused me to be mute. I was not a man who did not know how to speak his native language. Instead, I was a man who knew how to speak two languages. I was a bilingual man who knew how to speak both English and French. You might think that my knowledge of two languages might have had me at a social advantage rather than a social disadvantage. Sadly, this was not the case though since my knowing two languages led me to being bullied and ridiculed. Then, this led me to developing social anxiety.

My social anxiety led me to developing a fear of being around people. I feared being around all people. It did not matter if these people were men, women, young people, old people, and their ethnicity did not matter either. This social discomfort was always present. The only difference was the level of discomfort that I felt around certain people. At the heart of this social discomfort, was my fear of confrontation. I had this fear of confrontation because I feared getting into fights or arguments with people. I feared getting into these fights or arguments with people for two reasons. One reason why I had this fear was obvious. It was because of my fear of being hurt or injured. The second reason was not so obvious. It was more about me reawakening my many years of being bullied and ridiculed during elementary and middle school.

This social discomfort I felt from the fear of confrontation led me to avoiding social situations. I avoided all social situations like the plague because it was my belief that all people were angry. It was also my belief that their anger needed an outlet. I believed that this outlet was to get into a confrontation with the first person to aggravate them. So, I avoided all social situations because I did not wish to be the one to aggravate someone into a confrontation. Avoiding social situations for fear of confrontation was what led me to living a life of isolation.

This life of isolation led me to developing a world of isolation. This world of isolation was the place where I went to avoid social situations. This world of isolation was the only place I felt safe from humanity. It was not always a needed escape though because there was a time from the age of five to ten when my social anxiety was nonexistent. I call these years, the years of "My Wonderful French Childhood", and they were the best years of my life. One reason why they were the best years of my life was because of my French culture. During the years of "My Wonderful French Childhood", I lived within a region of France filled with Celtic pride. I lived here because of my French grandparents from my father's side of the family. My French grandparents owned a farm which they called "Les Isles De Plouisy". "Les Isles De Plouisy" helped me to create "My Wonderful French Childhood" since we were so isolated from people. Yet, we were also not that isolated because we were constantly being visited by people. We were constantly being visited by people because of my French Grandmother. My French grandmother had this gift of making me and everyone else around her feel socially comfortable.

My wonderful French grandmother was one of the reasons why my social anxiety was nonexistent during "My Wonderful French Childhood". My two best friends were also a part of the reason why my social anxiety was nonexistent. My two best friends during "My Wonderful French Childhood" were Annabelle and Pierre-Yves. Annabelle was one of my best friends, and it did not matter that she was a girl. This shows how truly nonexistent my social anxiety was during "My Wonderful French Childhood". My other best friend was

Pierre-Yves, who was my favorite French cousin of four because we were the same age and loved reading comics. The last of these four individuals to keep my social anxiety at bay was my French grandfather. My French grandfather was the fun grandparent, he was the one I loved being around before developing social anxiety. Then, I developed social anxiety and my French grandmother turned into the fun grandparent because I was so socially comfortable around her. These four individuals had me believing my social anxiety did not exist. They gave me a glimpse into what life might have been like if I was able to socialize with anyone at any time. I believed this path was a future of true happiness because it was going to lead me to the woman of my dreams. Sadly, once I left "My Wonderful French Childhood", I saw my life of true happiness disappear.

I had to adapt to my new life of living with social anxiety. I had to accept that "My Wonderful French Childhood" was gone when I left France. I never did fully recover from this devastating loss. Today, anytime that I hear a beautiful French song I am instantly transported back to "My Wonderful French Childhood". Once there, I think about how great my life could have been if I had never left France. For starters, I believe I could have always had social support from my grandfather, grandmother, Pierre-Yves, and Annabelle. Then, I believe this social support could have helped me make new friends. Sometimes I even believe that this social support is something that may have led me to a life where my social anxiety did not exist.

I believe that taking the path of "My Wonderful French Childhood" might have led me toward one of two futures. One future could have been the path of me marrying Annabelle since I believe that Annabelle was my French soul mate. I also believe that this path could have led to Pierre-Yves still being alive because I could have been there to support him when he needed it. Then, he could have been the best man at my wedding. Another future could have been one where Annabelle and Pierre Yves remained my good friends. Then with the support of their friendships, I could have met an unknown beauty who could have been my wife. I believe that either of these paths could have led to a future of true happiness. Then, I believe both of these paths might have led me to a life of getting married and having a family. I believe a life of marriage and having a family is the path every man hopes to attain someday, if they are so lucky.

I was not going to be one of these lucky men. I saw my future of true happiness slip away the moment I learned we had to leave France. I saw it slip away because once I left "My Wonderful French Childhood", I started developing my social anxiety. The loss of "My Wonderful French Childhood" was a turning point for the way I was to live the rest of my life. It was the difference of me believing I had no trouble talking to people, or of me believing that I was never going to be able to socialize with people. Eventually, I was going to follow this new path of living with social anxiety toward my passion for writing. However, this path toward my passion for writing did not present itself for another thirty-one years. During these thirty-one years, I was going to have to learn how to live with the social discomfort of social anxiety. This social discomfort is the focus of the rest of this chapter. During the remaining pages of this chapter, I will introduce a few of the major life events which led to me developing social anxiety.

The first major event that led to me developing social anxiety was the loss of "My Wonderful French Childhood". Once I left France, I had to adjust to my new life. I had to adapt to the American culture. I found that making this adjustment was going to be very difficult and uncomfortable. This was because as soon as I started school I was bullied and ridiculed. Elementary school kicked off my years of being bullied and ridiculed for many different reasons.

I was mostly ridiculed during elementary school. I was ridiculed for having a French accent. I was ridiculed for both my middle and last name. I was ridiculed for crying, although I never cried again after Elementary school. I remember sitting at my grandmother's funeral and not shedding a tear. Even years later, when I lost my third book, I still did not shed a tear. I felt the urge to cry. However, right as my tears rose out of me, I absorbed them like a Bounty towel. Finally, I was ridiculed for being shy. The more I was being ridiculed by everyone during elementary school, the more sensitive I was toward any type of negative criticism. Thus, when it was finally time to graduate elementary school and leave, I was so excited. I was so excited because

I was looking forward to escaping what I thought were the worst years of my childhood.

My middle school years turned out to be the worst years of my childhood. My middle school years were the worst years because they were so detrimental to my social development. I never fully recovered from the pain I felt from being both bullied and ridiculed during middle school. I attended two middle schools during middle school. The first middle school that I attended was not safe at all. I remember it as being a high school from one of those old eighties' movies where a teacher or principal arrived to save the school. It reminded me of *Lean on Me* and *The Principal*. My school was not actually this bad. However, this was the way I remembered it because of all the bullying that I had to endure while I was at this middle school.

There was the time when one of my peers turned around to hit me for some unknown reason. It was right at the start of class when I was hit. I did not have any friends for social support, so all I could do was sit there. As I was sitting there, I started thinking about what I might have done to provoke him. I could not think of what I did though, so eventually I stopped caring about what I did to provoke him because I cared more about how embarrassed I felt. These feelings of embarrassment consumed my every thought during class. I felt so uncomfortable during class because of these thoughts that I created an invisible man complex.

I started seeing how much time I could go without saying a word to anyone. Hours turned to days. Days turned to weeks. I got really good at being invisible. Then, I was able to switch middle schools when my parents moved. At first, I was thinking how wonderful it was going to be to start over since it meant my years of being bullied and ridiculed were over. Then, I found out they were not over, merely the type of abuse was going to change. It went from physical abuse to emotional abuse. It was at my second middle school that a rumor was going to spread about my being gay. I did not know about this rumor until I graduated. Before graduating, I only knew that I was being shunned which strengthened my invisible man complex.

It was during my middle school years that I learned of the magic of skipping school. Skipping school gave me an escape from the pain I was feeling from being bullied and ridiculed. After all, how could I be bullied and ridiculed if I was not present to be bullied and ridiculed. Unfortunately, skipping school was always only a temporary escape from the social discomfort of my social anxiety. I knew I had to return to school because it was what the rest of humanity expected. So eventually, I always returned to school and to the anxiety of having to be around people. This return also meant a return to my invisible complex. This invisible man complex was the only way I knew how to deal with humanity since I did not believe I could socialize. Thus, my invisible man complex was my means of survival when skipping school was not possible. Eventually, this invisible man complex was going to turn into my world of isolation.

My first escape into my world of isolation was with television. Saturday morning cartoons were the first shows that offered me my escape. Saturday mornings I was watching *The Snorks*, *The Smurfs*, *Alvin and The Chipmunks*, and *The Looney Tunes Hour*. Yet, *The Smurfs* were what I was the most excited about watching. As I got older, the shows I watched were going to be teen shows and I believe these teen shows were my first taste of beautiful celebrities.

I was able to return to reality enough to graduate middle school. My years of being bullied and ridiculed were over. Unfortunately, this did not mean that the damage I felt from being bullied and ridiculed was over. As I started high school, my invisible man complex and my world of isolation were an even more powerful way to escape. Luckily, I had some friends who could help me feel somewhat socially comfortable during high school. There was one group of friends who invited me to parties and clubs to help me get out of my shell. Sadly, my invisible man complex stopped me from taking advantage of going to these events. I did eventually meet one person I was able to feel socially comfortable with outside of the group.

My friends helped me to have a temporary escape from my social anxiety. I say temporary escape because I was still skipping school during high school. I was also still turning to my invisible man complex and my world of isolation when I was around them. I hated my social anxiety and all I dreamed of while going to high school was returning to France. I wanted nothing more than to return to a time when my social anxiety was nonexistent. I so wanted to return to "My Wonderful French Childhood". I was finally going to get this chance after high school. After graduation, my father told me that he was going to be sending me to France for about seven months. I was very excited to learn that I was returning to France because I thought this meant I was finally going to return to "My Wonderful French Childhood". Sadly, once I returned to France, I was going to learn that I was only returning to France. This did not mean a return to a time when my social anxiety did not exist. When I returned to France, I was able to temporarily reconnect with my French grandparents and my two best friends. However, my reconnection did not last because my social anxiety was too much a part of who I was to ignore.

I returned from France feeling very depressed and anxious. I was feeling depressed because I knew that my dream of returning to "My Wonderful French Childhood" was over. I was feeling anxious because now I knew there was no escaping my anxiety. Also, I felt this anxiety because I was not sure what I was going to do with the rest of my life. I did not know how I was going make it through the rest of my life with my social anxiety. I believed that this social anxiety was going to keep me out of work. My lack of work meant that I was never going to be able to save any money. This meant that I could never find the financial means to move away from my parents. Finally, this meant never having a romantic relationship since no woman wants to be with a man who still lives with his parents. It is not that I did not try to find employment and move away from my parents. Sadly, though, I was unsuccessful every time.

I spent about five years trying to move away from my parents. I found and quit employment too many times for me to count. I joined the marines and graduated from boot camp. Then, once I returned after a ten-day leave, I found a way to get myself medically discharged. I went to community college thinking getting an education might be the answer. However, I could not choose a major. So, I quit because I had no passion or direction while attending. Finally, I tried to move away from my parents several times as I tried to get employment. Yet, every time I tried, I failed and moved back because of my social anxiety.

The last time I tried to move away from my parents' home was when I moved to Florida with my best friend. My best friend was great because he understood me better than anyone else. Sadly, as supportive as he was, I still could not keep work because of my social anxiety. So, I returned to Ohio feeling defeated and depressed. I felt there was no escaping my future of living with my parents, so I quit trying. Once I stopped trying, I had to start to accept that I was never going to be able to escape my debilitating social anxiety. I started to accept that the only two relationships I was going to have were going to be my parents. I had to accept this dark reality.

Television was my only escape from this dark reality. Television was the only thing I cared about for about a year. My year of television lasted from December of the year 2000 until February of 2002. I had each and every hour planned out for watching television. Every Sunday, I got the TV Guide and I studied it as if it was the bible. Every weekday at three, I watched *Guiding Light*. Every weekday at five, I watched *the X-Files*. Every night, I watched my new primetime shows. Every Saturday, I watched SYFY shows all day. I spent my Saturdays watching *Relic Hunter, Andromeda, Star Trek, Sheena,* and *She Spies*. This escape into the world of television worked great for me for about a year. Then, after about a year, television was starting to lose its magic. It was losing its magic because of the arguments I was getting into with my parents. My parents did not understand how I could sit around all day watching television. They did not understand because they never understood my social anxiety.

We were getting into arguments every night which was causing me to feel very guilty about not working. This guilt meant the loss of television as my escape from the darkness I felt was my reality. It meant a return to my debilitating social anxiety. I had no clue how I was going to move forward without television. I knew I could not socialize with people and it was killing me inside. I could not talk to my parents about this since they were too angry about me not working and paying rent. I understood their anger and I wanted to make money. Unfortunately, even though I truly wanted to, I could not get work because of my social anxiety.

I could not take it anymore! I needed some help! I started looking through the phone book for emergency phone numbers or something. I was not sure what I was looking for. I only knew what I was doing was not working. I knew that television had lost its magic. So, as I was looking through the phone book, I found a phone number for Portage Path. I never heard of Portage Path before. So, I was not sure what made me call them. I guess it was my desperation.

My journey with Portage Path started with them getting me out of the house. I was finding it very difficult to leave the house. I still find it difficult to leave the house. I remember my therapist had to call me several times to get me out of the house. Somehow, I was able to finally get out of the house and gradually return to reality. Once I started leaving the house more, the following step was for me to get employment. My first venture back to the world of work was at this call center where you surveyed people. I did not love this work. Yet, I tolerated doing this work for about a year and a half. I worked there from about 2003 to 2005.

I was fired from this call center at the start of the summer of 2005. I started to think about finding my own place before getting fired because I was starting to get a savings account. Then, once I was fired, and lost my financial means to move out. This led me to some soul searching about what I was going to do with my future. I started talking to my therapist about my love for learning and wanting to go back to college. He supported me and encouraged me to go back to college. This was not a great decision for me financially because my financial loan debt will follow me for the rest of my life. I believe this debt has made it impossible for me to ever move out because I have such bad credit. However, I am not able to say I regret my decision to go to college since my five years at college allowed me time to cultivate my writing.

"You have been accepted to The University of Anchorage!" I could not believe the words I was reading. This was the best news of my life at the time. I had actually been accepted to the graduate school that was my number one choice of attending. There was no way I could have been accepted to the graduate school of my dreams. Yet, I was, and I was only one of ten students to be accepted. The best part of me being accepted though was my reason for being accepted. I never took the entrance exams or even went for an interview. My GPA was good, yet nothing that great. I had a 3.5 GPA. Thus, I knew that there was only one reason I was accepted to The University of Anchorage. I knew I was accepted because of my college essay.

This only strengthened the confidence I felt for my passion for writing. I was unbelievably excited about going to Alaska. Unfortunately, my being accepted to the University of Anchorage also meant taking a break from my passion for writing. I only moved to Alaska for about three months. I returned to Ohio feeling defeated because I lost my dream of moving to Alaska. After returning to Ohio, I returned to work at a retail store and two call centers. However, my social anxiety had me feeling so defeated that I could not find a way to keep work.

Beautiful Women

This is the story of a man who is consumed by his thoughts of beautiful women. I am rarely able to get through a single minute without thinking about a beautiful woman. I will either be thinking about trying to get a look at them if they are present or how to get one if not present. My thoughts of seeing or being with a beautiful woman will consume about 95% of my thoughts.

I was going to work wondering if one of my beautiful angels from work was working or not. The presence of one of these angels at work was going to help me decide what type of day I was going to have at work. I was either going to have a great day if I was able to see her or vice versa if not. Then, after work, I thought about where to go to see the most beautiful women. I was either going to be spending my time at the library or at the French Bistro. I went to the library between the hours of four to eight, then I spent the rest of my time at the French Bistro.

I started keeping a schedule of the beautiful angels at the library when I started my spiritual journey. I started keeping track of my angels by first keeping track of the times when my beautiful blonde library angel was at the nearby library. I did not want to miss a single moment of seeing her there. Then, I discovered the other library angels working there and I started to keep track of them as well. As I kept track of them,

I also started to rank them. Obviously, the beautiful blonde library angel was at the top of the list and then the rest followed. During the first year of my spiritual journey, the library was my only location of inspiration. Then, I found the angels at the French Bistro and I now had two locations of inspiration. The French Bistro was a great addition since it helped me to find more angels of inspiration. My thoughts were now consumed by all the beautiful angels from the library and the French Bistro.

My thoughts of beautiful women continued to consume me when I got home at nights because when I got home, I started to dream about them. I was dreaming about the life I wish I could have with any one of these beautiful angels that I was obsessing over. I called these dreams my real dreams because when I had them, they felt so real. My real dreams were about everyday events. One dream was about me simply riding the bus and talking to Taylor Swift. Then, another was about me sitting by the pool with the beautiful blonde library angel. These real dreams were never about anything that special. They were simply about things I wish I could do with beautiful women if I was able to talk to them. After I was to reawaken from my real dreams, I fell into a dark state of depression because I realized they were not real. Yet, I could not stop thinking how much I wished these real dreams could somehow have been real life.

This was the life of a man consumed by his thoughts of beautiful women. These beautiful women could have been my age or younger. They could have been blonde, brunette, black-haired, or redheaded. They could have been friendly, mean, shy, or outgoing. The personality of these beautiful women did not matter since I could not talk to them. My inability to speak to beautiful women made everything about them a mystery other than their beauty. The most I could hope to say was the occasional hello or I think you look beautiful today. My inability to speak to them while still thinking about them so much led to me obsessing over them.

My first object of obsession was this young blonde from elementary school. There was not much I remembered about this blonde beauty other than her wearing her hair as a ponytail. I must have found her very attractive though if I developed an obsession with her. I was so obsessed with her that I wanted to propose to her. I asked my grandmother for an engagement ring for Christmas, then I wrote her a love note and I placed it upon her desk. Then, I hid behind a door to eavesdrop as she read the note to her friends. Then, I heard them all laughing. This was my first experience of being hurt by beautiful women. After this painful experience, I turned to my obsession with celebrities because my obsession with them had no repercussions.

Over my years of obsessing over beautiful women, I obsessed over celebrities and real girls equally because I believed it was impossible to talk to them. So, I only cared about their beauty.

The first celebrity that I obsessed over was Alyssa Milano. My obsession with her has faded away. However, I will always remember her as my first celebrity obsession. Every night, I was looking forward to watching *Who's the Boss?* I think my favorite thing about Alyssa Milano was her curly brunette hair. She was one of my many obsessions with beautiful celebrities. After my obsession with Alyssa Milano, my obsession with celebrities continued.

Shania Twain and Jennifer Love Hewitt were going to be my primary celebrity obsessions. Jennifer Love Hewitt was the first of my two celebrity obsessions. She was this beautiful brunette with an amazing body and a great smile. Her smile was what I was obsessed over because it represented her smiling personality which was my favorite thing about her. She was a celebrity who appeared to always be very cheerful. Every time I saw her doing interviews she was giggling and smiling, and I loved this side of her personality. I could never understand how she could always be so cheerful, though, because of my social anxiety. She was most famous for *Party of Five*, although I never really watched this show other than to see her beauty.

Most of my time spent obsessing over Jennifer Love Hewitt consisted of pictures from magazines and calendars. I could not get enough of seeing her and learning about her life. I read her autobiography and I was probably one of the few people to buy all her CDs. I was actually someone who felt that she could have had a better singing career than a career as an actress. I always felt she could have had a better singing career because she had such a beautiful voice. I was so obsessed with her that at one point, I even thought about going to Hollywood to find her. However, this thought never really went beyond the idea stage. The reason why it never went beyond the idea stage was not that she was so famous, nor the distance between us. It was more my social anxiety. I did not believe I could socialize with her even if I got to Hollywood. Therefore, there was no point of going. This did not mean my obsession with her was over though, because my obsession with her continued until I found a new celebrity obsession. Before I found a new celebrity obsession though, there was a beautiful blonde from high school.

My new object of obsession after Jennifer Love Hewitt was this beautiful blonde from high school. This beautiful blonde girl from high school was the closest I was ever going to get to having a real girlfriend. Granted, this was never very close, although for a man suffering from social anxiety who has never had a romantic relationship it was very close. My relationship with her started when I got a note from her at my work. This beautiful blonde girl from the food court had actually taken the time to tell me that she found me physically attractive. She was the first and only beautiful woman to ever take the time to let me know how she felt. This was something that took a great deal of courage since we had never spoken before. Thus, there was no mystery as to how she felt because her letter told me everything. Unfortunately, I did not have a clue what to do once I got the letter because I did not have anyone I could go to for advice at the time.

I did not have any friends because this was before I met my group of friends. I did not know my best friend since I met him through my group of friends. Also, my father was always working, so I could not ask him for advice. I never spoke to my mother about women because we rarely spoke about anything. Also, this was before I knew of therapy. Thus, I had no clue what to do once I got this letter from her. Yet, I still tried since she was beautiful and interested.

My first attempt to approach her was a success because I was able to speak to her and eventually get her phone number. I could not believe I had gotten her phone number. I called her that night and was even more excited when I learned that it was her real number. After calling this beautiful angel, we spoke for a few more minutes. Then, my social anxiety started to make its appearance, so I told her I had to get off the phone to do some vacuuming. Unfortunately, I never spoke to her again after I got off the phone this time. So, I was thinking that I lost my chance with her. Then, a few months passed, and I approached her again. We again spoke for a few minutes and I got her phone number. Then, sadly, the same series of events happened again. Finally, a few months passed, and I made one last attempt at dating her.

This beautiful blonde from high school must have been interested because I had about four chances at dating her during high school. I was never going to date her since I did not know how to date a woman. Yet, it still felt wonderful knowing she was interested, and I had a chance with her. The last chance I had with her was Valentine's Day when I sent her a rose. Again, I was unsuccessful because I also sent a rose to her friend. Then, her friend approached me after getting the rose to tell me I might have had a chance with her if I had not sent them both a rose. Once the beautiful brunette told me this, I thought I lost any chance that I had of dating her. However, a few months later I saw her outside of Blockbuster Video and we spoke again, and I was thinking I might still have a chance with her. This was the last time that I ever saw my beautiful blonde from high school, and this was the closest I ever got to having a real girlfriend.

My beautiful blonde angel from high school was my first obsession with a beautiful woman who was not a celebrity. I could not stop thinking about this beautiful blonde from high school after she wrote me a letter to tell me that she was interested. These thoughts turned into my first obsession when I started driving because I found out what car she was driving. I knew she drove a black Camaro. This then turned into my dream car because she was driving it and because it was a nice car. Once I learned what car she drove, I also found out where she lived. So, I knew where she lived and what car she drove. Yet, I did nothing with any of this information because of my social anxiety. All I could do was obsess over what might have been if I could only socialize with her. During my two-year obsession with her, I was constantly listening to Phil Collins "Both Sides of the Story". This Phil Collins album evolved into the theme music to my obsession with her. This obsession with her was going to last until I graduated high school. It continued until I returned to France and I reconnected with Annabelle.

I had one magical and very real day with Annabelle when I returned to France. We walked around the old traditional streets of Guingamp talking for about two hours. I am not sure I remember what we spoke about as we walked around these old traditional streets. Yet, what I do remember is how I felt and how I forgot all about time during this walk. I never felt more comfortable talking to a beautiful woman than I did this day. I was able to joke with her and talk to her about anything. We never stopped talking. This day was truly magical and a day that I will never forget because it was so real as well. After this magical day, I started to consider her my French soulmate. Then, more recently, I started thinking of the beautiful blonde from high school as being my American soul mate. I felt very comfortable talking to Annabelle. Time flew by and two hours felt like two minutes. Unfortunately, this was the only day I had with her.

I called her to say goodbye after this very real and magical day. I called to tell her goodbye because I had decided to return to America unless I thought I had a chance with her. I was hoping to feel the magic of this very real day again with her when I called. Unfortunately, the magic was not there, and this was the last time that we ever spoke. After I returned to America, I wrote her a letter to let her know how I felt. However, we were oceans apart when I wrote it, and I knew my time with her was over. I still had a flicker of hope left after writing her the letter that maybe someday we might find our way to each other. Then, I learned that she got married and that flicker of hope was lost forever. I then had learned that Pierre-Yves had committed suicide and my grandparents died around this same time. So, not only did I lose my French soulmate, I also lost "My Wonderful French Childhood". These two losses were devastating losses because I also believed I had lost my chances of ever finding true happiness.

Annabelle was a very special obsession because she was the only beautiful angel I obsessed over during the best years of my life. She was also the last real girl I obsessed over for many years. It took me about fifteen years to find another real beautiful woman to obsess over. So, after Annabelle, I returned to my obsession with beautiful celebrities. I found my new celebrity obsession while I was walking around the mall one day thinking about my new path.

Shania Twain was my new object of obsession. I first discovered Shania Twain while walking into a music store to listen to "Come on Over". Once I heard her album, I forgot about what I was thinking about as I was walking around the mall. After I heard her album, all I cared about was listening to her music and her beautiful voice. Thus, started my obsession with the talented and beautiful Shania Twain. I fell in love with every song from "Come on Over" and my favorite song was "You're Still The One." After discovering Shania Twain, I started listening to all her music. Also, I bought every magazine and calendar that had a picture of her.

I also read her autobiography which I found very inspirational. Shania Twain had lost both her parents and she had to raise her brothers and sisters by herself. She did all of this while continuing to pursue her passion for music. Shania Twain was inspirational, beautiful, successful, and diverse. One could see her diversity with her music since it was a crossover of rock and country music. During my time of obsessing over Shania Twain, I bought all her CDs and did not stop listening to her music for about a year. Sadly, after a year of listening to her music my excitement for her music faded away because I overplayed it. However, any time I hear her music I am reminded of my obsession with her. I believe that Shania Twain is the closest thing to a perfect celebrity that will ever exist. Thus, after my obsession with her, I never found another single celebrity to obsess over. Instead, I started to obsess over a variety of different beautiful celebrities. However, none of these celebrities held a candle to Shania Twain.

My obsession with female celebrities was solely based upon their looks. I was so obsessed with the beauty of female celebrities because there were so many of them. This great variety of female celebrities to obsess over led me to start keeping track of them. I started ranking the beauty of all of these female celebrities. Ranking them became a favorite past time of mine, especially when I was bored at work. When bored at work, I started my shift by making a list of a hundred beautiful celebrities. Then, once I finished making the list of a hundred celebrities, I started to eliminate a female celebrity as each minute of work passed. I eliminated beautiful celebrities until ten celebrities remained. Yet, my top ten list of beautiful celebrities never really changed much.

Brooke Burke, Sarah Alexander, Kristen Miller, Kristen Kreuk, Laura Vandervoort, Jamie Chung, Jeri Ryan, April Bowlby, Rachel Bilson, and Sophie Marceau. These were always the ten most beautiful women. The order never really changed much either and Brooke Burke and Sarah Alexander were always the top two. My obsession with female celebrities helped fill the void of not having a real relationship or any real women to obsess over.

The University of Akron paved the way for my return to obsessing over real women. I never had one single beautiful woman to obsess over at the university. So, I was spending most of my time at the university obsessing over a variety of beautiful women. Then, all of this changed when I was accepted to The University of Anchorage and I found a new real obsession.

My new object of obsession at The University of Anchorage was this beautiful tanned brunette angel from Texas. This Texas angel was probably the most beautiful angel I have ever been obsessed over. However, as beautiful as she was, it was not her beauty that made her so special. What made her so special, was how sweet and friendly she was because every time she saw me, she was saying hello with this bright Texas smile. It did not matter if it was when we crossed paths outside of class or during class, she was always saying hello. This made her very approachable. This approachability was helping me find the confidence to socialize with her. Unfortunately, I had to leave Alaska and this Texas angel which meant finding a new obsession.

My new object of obsession was a Mexican beauty I met when I started to work at a factory. I never imagined talking to this Mexican beauty because I knew I could not instigate a conversation with her. Then, she started instigating the conversations with me and we were talking to each other every time we worked together. I could not believe I was able to talk to her when I could not talk to anyone else at or outside of work. The best day we spent together was when we spent twelve hours socializing. We never stopped talking to each other during these twelve hours. For that one special day, I forgot all about my inability to talk to beautiful women. Even during our lunch hour, we sat together and kept talking to each other. The only time I felt my social anxiety was when I had to approach her at the start of the shift. Unfortunately, this relationship never went beyond work because I lost her phone number after leaving this factory.

My memories of her led me to my obsession with this Mexican beauty. It was a few months after I left this factory when I had these memories of her. My memories of her returned when I was driving to my new work at another factory. During my drive to work, I was going to hear a Mana song called "Bendita Tu Luz" or Blessed the Light when translated to English. This song brought back all these memories of this Mexican beauty and led me to another magical day with her. Except this time, it was all imagined. I referred to this day with her memories as my magical Saturday. My magical Saturday started when I heard this Mana Song. Once I got to work, my fear was that these memories might leave once I got out of the car. However, these memories of this Mexican beauty never faded away. Instead, they intensified after I got to work.

My memories of my Mexican beauty intensified after I got to work because I heard another beautiful Spanish song that kept her memories alive. This other Spanish song was going to be a Spanish song by Chayanne. The song was called "Yo Te Amo." After hearing this song, my memories of her were even more powerful and they remained the entire day. So, my entire day at work I was feeling a state of joy that was inspired by my memories of her. Once I got to work, this song and my memories of her were helping me to cope with the difficulties of work. I heard this song over and over within my mind and remembered our talks at work. Finally, I got home after my shift and I wrote about this magical day that I had with her memories. Then, I started to write her a letter to tell her how I felt. I knew that I could not send her this letter. However, what this did do was offer me a glimpse into the spiritual energy of beautiful women.

My passion for writing might be my only way to express the feelings that I have for beautiful women. I may never have the courage or confidence to approach them and talk to them because of my debilitating social anxiety. This is something I might have to learn to accept. This means that my obsessions with these beautiful women might be the only relationships that I will ever know with them. Beautiful women have always been the most intimidating creatures I have ever known. I always believed that I could not talk to beautiful women, and that this

Mexican beauty and Annabelle were only exceptions to the rule. The rest of my life had been all about my obsessions with them since I was still mesmerized by their beauty. Then, I found the beautiful blonde library angel and she introduced me to my passion for writing. This passion for writing was helping me find the confidence to question my beliefs. The more time I spent with my passion for writing, the more I found examples of times when I could talk to them. My passion for writing helped me to see that I had been blocking out these memories. I was blocking out these memories since I wanted to find a way to avoid my socially anxious thoughts.

My Socially Anxious Thoughts

This chapter takes a look at my socially anxious thoughts. These socially anxious thoughts are my reason for living a life afraid of everyone and everything. I am afraid of men. I am afraid of women. I am afraid of mean people. I am afraid of nice people. I am afraid of my parents. I am afraid of all the members of my family who are not my parents. I am afraid of my supervisors at work. I am afraid of customers and my coworkers. I am afraid of being around people. I am afraid of being alone. I am afraid of death. I am afraid of life. I am afraid of being invisible. I am afraid of being visible. I live my life always afraid of someone or something. Thus, this is why I have been living my life isolated and alone and within my world of isolation.

My world of isolation was the only place where I felt safe from humanity. I needed this escape from humanity because humanity is my reason for having these socially anxious thoughts. I feel this world is cruel and unsympathetic to someone living with social anxiety. Thus, I choose to spend as much time as I am able to within my world of isolation because humanity does not exist within this world. Whenever

I enter my world of isolation, I am able to let go of all my worries, fear, anger, and sadness. So, I never want to leave the safety of my world of isolation. Sadly, I have to leave this world of isolation at times to return to my world of reality.

I have to return to my world of reality to go to the library. I have to return to go to the French Bistro. I have to return to go to work. Finally, I have to return to get home. This return to reality is something that I always dreaded doing since it meant leaving my world of safety. There is only one thing that inspires me to want to leave this world and that is the hope of attaining a beautiful woman. Beautiful women are the only thing that make my life outside of my world of isolation worth living. I live my life with the hope of one day building the confidence to approach and talk to a beautiful woman. Sadly, I know this is something that will never happen from within my world of isolation. It takes me a great deal of energy to muster enough courage to confront my social anxiety and leave my world of isolation. I am much more comfortable spending hours at a time within my world of isolation. However, once I see a beautiful woman my anxiety will disappear for a brief moment and I am able to return to reality.

My love for beautiful women has no limits. I am attracted to beautiful women of any age. This even includes younger women which sometimes makes me very uncomfortable. Yet, I know I am unable to speak to them because of my social anxiety. Hence, this discomfort will usually fade away quickly. One day as I was working, I remember seeing one of these beautiful young angels. I did not know her exact age, although I knew she was way too young for me to be having these thoughts of her. I could not stop myself though because this young brunette had one of the cutest faces I had ever seen. I could not get enough of seeing the cute face of this young brunette. Then, as she started approaching my cart, I was feeling my anxiety increase more and more until she finally got to my cart. I had no idea how to act once she reached my cart because of my debilitating social anxiety. The more I stared at this young brunette angel with the cutest face, the more I got scared and anxious. My fear was that someone might see me staring at her and say something about me staring at her. Most of my fear and anxiety though was about her actually being interested because then she might want to socialize. I knew that this was most likely not going to happen, yet this fear and anxiety was still present. It makes no difference what the age is of these beautiful women because my social anxiety is always present. Finally, this young brunette angel with the cutest face I had ever seen left and once she finally left, I felt some relief from my social anxiety. Unfortunately, this relief later turned into a dark state of depression because I knew I was most likely never going to see her again. These thoughts of a young brunette angel are only a sample of my many thoughts of beautiful women.

My thoughts of beautiful women are why I feel I am not able to speak to people. How am I supposed to speak to people when all I think about is beautiful women? Yet, the thoughts I have of beautiful women do not disappear if I never speak to people. It only keeps them hidden from people because I do not want to be judged or criticized for having them. I did not believe that anyone could ever understand me having these thoughts and doing nothing about them. Thus, most of my fear and anxiety is of people criticizing me for not being able to act upon my thoughts of beautiful women. My fear of others criticizing me are not my only reason for keeping my thoughts of beautiful women hidden. There are other reasons why I am hiding them.

I hide my thoughts of beautiful women because I fear the competitive nature of men. I hide these thoughts because I fear talking to beautiful women if they learn I am interested. I hide my thoughts because I fear how the parents will react if they learn I find their children attractive. All of these thoughts are constantly running through my mind after I see beautiful women. So, the brief moments of joy I get from seeing beautiful women are followed by a rush of anxiety. This anxiety goes away when they leave though, and then it is followed by my dark depression.

This state of depression makes it difficult for me to socialize with people since I feel everyone else is able to comfortably socialize with beautiful women. This then leads me to a life where I feel isolated and alone. This leads me to a life where I feel as if no one will ever understand the uniqueness of my life. I have tried talking to my therapists about my thoughts of beautiful women which does help me when I see them. Unfortunately, I only see my therapist once a month, or if I am really lucky every two weeks. The rest of the time I will keep these thoughts hidden since I fear being ridiculed and criticized for my thoughts of beautiful women.

I choose to keep all my thoughts of beautiful women hidden. I choose to keep my thoughts of my beautiful blonde library angel hidden. I choose to hide my thoughts of beautiful celebrities. I choose to hide my thoughts of the beautiful women working and eating at the French Bistro. I choose to hide my thoughts of the beautiful women I have been obsessed over throughout my life. All of these choices have led me to developing my debilitating social anxiety. My debilitating social anxiety turned me into a man without a voice. Then, I discovered the beautiful blonde library angel and she introduced me to the magic of the library.

The magic of the library was going to be my safe haven where I could go every day to cultivate my passion for writing. My passion for writing allowed me to have a safe place to go where I could express all my thoughts about beautiful women. My passion for writing was taking away the shame that I felt for having these thoughts and turned them into my inspiration.

My beautiful blonde library angel and the magic of the library introduced me to my passion for writing. My passion for writing introduced me to the power of my obsession with beautiful women. This obsession with beautiful women gave birth to my spiritual journey. Eventually, this spiritual journey helped me to realize the story of the first book I was to publish.

The beauty of my beautiful blonde library angel inspired me to write my first book because she introduced me to the power of beautiful women. I found that this power increased with the library angels when she was not present. Then, it increased even more when I was surrounded by beautiful women at the French Bistro. I was surrounded by these beautiful women as I was writing about my socially anxious thoughts at the French Bistro. There were both beautiful women working there and eating there. There was a tall beautiful blonde supervisor working there. There was an equally beautiful, yet shorter beautiful blonde employee working there. There were these four young athletic angels eating there. Finally, there was this beautiful brunette customer who was also present. There I was at the French Bistro being surrounded by all these angels as I was trying to write my first book. Yet, all I wanted to do was stare at them. It was especially difficult for me to not stare at the four athletic angels because they were wearing shorts and T-shirts. All these beautiful angels made it quite difficult to focus.

I could not focus because I was too mesmerized by the beauty of these women working and eating at the French Bistro. I had this same trouble a while ago when this beautiful brunette with glasses was eating there. This brunette angel was one of the most beautiful women I ever saw. At least, I thought she was one of the most beautiful women that I ever saw at that moment. I realize that I say this about most of the beautiful angels I obsess over, and I really do believe this at the time when I see them because they are all so very beautiful. At the time of writing about the beautiful blonde library angel, she was one of the most beautiful women I ever saw. Yet, when I obsessed over the beautiful blonde from high school, she was the most beautiful. Then, as I was obsessing over Annabelle, I thought she was the most beautiful. I felt the same way about the Texas angel from Alaska. Lastly, I also felt this about the Mexican beauty. Hence, I am not sure who was the most beautiful all I knew was that they were all very beautiful.

I believe this beautiful brunette with glasses who was eating at the French Bistro was probably there for an interview. This angel with glasses chose to sit right within my line of sight when she first arrived at the French Bistro. At first, I was excited about where she chose to sit. Then, my excitement turned into excruciating anxiety since I could not stop thinking about her beauty. The anxiety that I was feeling made it nearly impossible for me to focus and write about this beautiful angel. This discomfort that I was feeling continued until the battery for my computer died and I had to move. I was not happy about having to move since it meant that I was not going to see this brunette angel anymore. Then, I found a place to sit where I could at least still see her hair. I even saw her entire face when she moved to get more comfortable. Finally, she left, and I fell into a state of depression since I knew this was one more angel I was never going to see again. This state of depression was always where I went to after my angels left since I knew these beautiful angels were not real. I knew they only lived within my writings.

My writings were creating a world where I found the confidence to start to build relationships with these beautiful angels that I was obsessing over. These relationships were only my obsessions with them. However, these obsessions were helping me to find the confidence to believe that I might one day socialize with them. My obsession with the beautiful blonde library angel was the most powerful of all these obsessions. My obsession with her was the most powerful since she introduced me to my passion for writing. My passion for writing was important because this was how I was starting to find my confidence. I found this confidence the more I was able to cultivate my passion for writing at my locations of inspiration.

My very first location of inspiration was my bedroom as a child. My bedroom was a great location of inspiration before I found the magic of beautiful women. Whenever I went to my bedroom, I could watch TV, listen to music, do puzzles, and play my video games. Then, after I discovered the magic of beautiful women, I left my bedroom to see them. I was still feeling safe within my bedroom. However, I feared what I may miss if I always remained there.

My first location of inspiration with the magic of beautiful women was the Fort Lauderdale Beach. I loved the Fort Lauderdale beach because of what the beautiful women wore at the beach. They mostly wore bikinis at the beach. This was a powerful source of eye candy for a man who loved nothing more than looking at beautiful women. I could not spend enough time at the beach looking at these beautiful women and their bikinis. Once I moved to Ohio, I needed a new location of inspiration. This new location of inspiration was the University of Akron. During my time at the university, I spent most of my time at the college campus obsessing over all of the beautiful women attending college. This was until I moved to Alaska.

It was not until I made the move to Alaska that I was to find another single object of obsession. My last single object of obsession was the beautiful blonde from high school who sent me a letter to tell me that she was interested. Then, I discovered the Texas angel when I made the move to Alaska and I found a new object of obsession. I still believe that this Texas angel might have been the most beautiful of all my angels, if only based upon looks. The only time I saw this Texas angel was during class. Thus, the college campus where I saw several other beautiful angels after class was serving as my location of inspiration outside of class. Sadly, I was only at the University of Alaska for about one semester, then I had to return to Ohio.

My return to Ohio meant the search for a new library angel and a new location of inspiration. This search was going to eventually lead me to truck driving and my fall into my pit of darkness. Then, this fall led me to the discovery of the beautiful blonde library angel. This discovery was the first element to the creation of my location of inspiration. The second element was going to be the introduction of my passion for writing as I went there to obsess over her. My passion for writing was the only way that I knew how to express my socially anxious thoughts. A third important element that created my world of isolation at my location of inspiration was my need to escape the heat. It was this need to escape the heat that first led me to the library and discovering this angel. Thus, my love for the cold was the third element to my world of isolation. The fourth element that helped me to enter my world of isolation was Pepsi. Finally, the most important element that was helping me create my world of isolation was my passion for music. I loved all types of music. I loved Rock, Classical, Jazz, Spanish, Celtic, African, Oriental, and New Age. However, my all-time favorite type of music to listen to was French music. I loved French music most of all because when I listened to it, I was able to reconnect with "My Wonderful French Childhood" through the power of the French language.

My world of isolation was my escape from the world I feared so much because of my social anxiety. I entered this world of isolation once I wore my headphones and started listening to my passion for music. Then, once I found the spiritual energy of the beautiful blonde library angel, my spiritual journey was born. Finally, when the temperatures were cool, and I had my Pepsi I was ready to remain within this world for hours at a time without any wish to ever leave.

My world of isolation was a powerful and creative way for me to escape my fear of having to socialize with humanity. It was a place where I could go to cultivate my passion for writing. Cultivating my passion for writing was important because it allowed me to meet my best friend. My best friend was going to be myself. By myself, I mean my true inner self. The moment I started to accept my social anxiety for what it was, which was my life's handicap. I started to find a way to maneuver my way through this world with it. Another thing the discovery of my true self helped me to look at was my past and how my social anxiety was born.

I knew my socially anxious thoughts did not simply appear from out of nowhere. They had to have originated from somewhere. My passion for writing allowed me to take a close look into the origins of my socially anxious thoughts. I learned that my socially anxious thoughts originated from a series of events that occurred throughout my life. This series of events were my years of being bullied and ridiculed during elementary and middle school. These years caused me to feel isolated and alone because the only person I could trust was myself. My isolation and loneliness then caused me to create my world of isolation. I created this world of isolation because of my fear of humanity. I did not want these fears, however they were always present. Death was the only way I saw of escaping my fears which was not a real option. Death was never an option since I did not believe that there was anything after we died. Hence, I feared death more than I feared my dark existence since I believed death meant a loss of all hope.

My passion for writing was the one thing that was giving me hope within my dark existence. I knew that when I was cultivating my passion for writing I was able to find my true happiness. I knew when I entered my world of isolation with my passion for writing and my obsessions with my beautiful angels, I was able to find my true happiness. I knew that when it was cold, and I had my Pepsi or unsweetened tea I found my true happiness. I knew that when I was not at work and I was able to enter my world of isolation I found my true happiness. Dreadfully, I had to work to make money which meant my dealing with all my anxious thoughts.

My socially anxious thoughts will start before I even leave the house. They will start before I even get out of bed because when I first awaken, I will think of my fears of humanity. I will think of the traffic I will have to deal with to get to work. Finally, I find a way to leave my bed, get dressed, leave the house for the day, and most of the time even get to work. Unfortunately, once I get to work, I have to deal with an entirely new batch of anxious thoughts.

I will now present an example of a typical day of work with my socially anxious thoughts. My day started with me learning that I was going to be working near a coworker I felt socially comfortable around. I was looking forward to having someone to talk to until I discovered how popular she was and that I could not talk to her. This led to my social anxiety and to me thinking of an escape. I started counting down the minutes until I could go to lunch and escape for about a half an hour. Once lunch time arrived, I was thinking about the best path I might take to get to my car. Then I finally reached my car and I had about a half an hour to be isolated from humanity. However, this was not enough time to get over my social anxiety because my social anxiety was still very present. I returned to work after my break for lunch and my social anxiety was so powerful that I thought about another escape. Unfortunately, I knew there was no escape from my anxiety until my shift was over. I knew all I could do now was find a way to sit with my social discomfort for the rest of my shift. My social anxiety was so uncomfortable that I felt like crying. Yet, I knew crying was not an option since it was the middle of the workday and no one knew what I was feeling. So, I was standing at my cart feeling so socially anxious from my thoughts that I reverted back to my invisible man complex.

I was so relieved to finally get through my workday. I was so relieved to escape the social anxiety I had been feeling at work. After work, all I could think about was going to my locations of inspiration and my world of isolation. Unfortunately, my days with my socially anxious thoughts were still not over. Yes, the worst part of the day was over. However, there were still going to be two more events that led to me having more of these thoughts. The first of these events happened when I went to see my beautiful library angels. First, I wanted to see if the angel from the gas station was working since, I wanted a Pepsi after work. Then, when I got to the library, I found the best place to sit where I could see my beautiful blonde library angel. Then, I started to listen to my music when a librarian approached me to tell me my music was playing for everybody to hear it. This was the first event that caused my socially anxious thoughts. It took me about ten to fifteen minutes to focus upon my writing after this happened.

I was only at the library for about an hour before they closed, and I left to go see the beautiful angels at the French Bistro. I found a great place to sit between two beautiful angels once I got there and I started to listen to some music. Then, once again I found out that my music was playing for everyone to hear and it was much worse because I made the angels move.

This chapter introduced you to some of my socially anxious thoughts. These thoughts were more negative since they were about my inability to socialize with beautiful women. My inability to socialize with beautiful women is what led me to my passion for writing. This passion for writing helped me fight my negative thoughts with the dream of my snowy log cabin.

My Snowy Log Cabin

My snowy log cabin is where I see myself living when I envision my future. I imagine this snowy log cabin being somewhere within the snowy mountains of Alaska. I believe Alaska is the perfect location for my snowy log cabin because it is one of the coldest places that exists. My motto for Alaska has always been that there are forty-nine states for those who love the heat, and only one for those who love the cold. I could never understand how people could love the heat so much when it made me feel so uncomfortable all the time. I also had a problem with people who complained about the cold so much, and I started to call these people Snow Babies.

I imagined myself looking out the windows of my snowy log cabin watching the snow fall. This was making me feel very relaxed and comfortable. The more relaxed and comfortable I was feeling, the more my creativity was starting to flow. The more my creativity was starting to flow, the more I was feeling the spiritual energy of my beautiful blonde library angel. This spiritual energy led me into my world of isolation. So, my cabin was my location of inspiration.

The path to my snowy log cabin started with me realizing the story of my first book. I realized this story once I thought my beautiful blonde library angel left the library forever. Once I realized the story of my first book, I started writing the first draft of *The Beautiful Blonde Library Angel*. As I wrote my first draft, I knew that I was taking another step toward my snowy log cabin. This step consisted of me working and saving the money I needed to get published. As I started working, I had to remember my reason for working. I had to remember that I did not want to lose the magic of the beautiful blonde library angel as I was making money. I had to find a way to balance my need for making money and my passion for writing. I was able to find this balance by creating a schedule for when my beautiful blonde library angel was working. Once I created a schedule, I started to pursue my passion for writing when she was at the library and work the days she was not at the library. I believed that writing and publishing *The Beautiful Blonde Library Angel* was my first step toward one day attaining my snowy log cabin.

I believed that by publishing my first book I was going to have the financial means to work less. This was going to allow me more time to write more books which I hoped to also get published. The one thing that I knew was not going to change throughout the pursuit of my snowy log cabin was my passion for writing. My passion for writing was going to continue to be my true passion until I was physically unable to write anymore. I even imagined myself still pursuing my passion for writing once I made the move to my snowy log cabin. I knew of only one thing that might keep me from my passion for writing at my snowy log cabin. The only thing that could keep me from my passion for writing while there was the woman of my dreams.

I imagined myself living at this snowy log cabin with the woman of my dreams. I imagined us sitting by the fireplace of this snowy log cabin listening to the crackling firewood. I could smell the smoky aroma of the firewood as it was burning. I could feel the warmth of the fire as the heat was keeping us warm by the fireplace. The sight of the dancing fire upon the logs was very soothing as we were both sitting by the fire enjoying our cups of warm tea. As we sat by the fire, we started to talk to each other about what we did during the day. She told me all about her day of socialization with her friends while I started telling her about all of my writing.

The physical appearance of the woman of my dreams was a mystery. She could have been someone I knew that I could not speak to, or she could have been someone I had not yet met. Even though, her physical appearance may have been a complete mystery her spiritual presence was not a mystery. One thing I loved about her spiritual presence was that she was choosing to spend her nights by the fireplace talking to me while I simply listened to her voice. This mysterious woman of my dreams was actually able to accept me as this socially awkward person. This was what I loved about this mysterious woman of my dreams. Thus, I never felt more comfortable than I did while sitting by the fireplace with this mysterious woman of my dreams.

We were sitting by the fireplace talking for several hours. This was how we enjoyed spending our nights together at our snowy log cabin. She was doing most of the talking which I did not mind because I preferred to listen to her sweet and soothing voice as she talked. While sitting there listening to her sweet and soothing voice, I was feeling grateful. I was feeling grateful because I had finally found a beautiful woman to be with at my snowy log cabin. I was also feeling grateful because I had finally found someone to be socially comfortable around. This social comfort that I was feeling may only have been when I was within her spiritual presence, yet this was enough because my social anxiety made me not want to be around others.

Who was this mysterious woman at my snowy log cabin? What did this mysterious woman look like? Could I have already met this beautiful woman and not spoken to her because of my social anxiety? Could this mysterious woman of my dreams be someone who has not crossed my path yet? Finally, how did I ever find the courage and confidence to approach this beautiful woman of my dreams if she did exist? These were only some of the questions I was asking myself when I was envisioning myself with the woman of my dreams. I did not know the answer to any of these questions because I was still not anywhere near attaining her. I still lacked the confidence to approach a beautiful woman and have a conversation with her. Sure, I could sometimes approach them and say hello or tell them they were beautiful. However, I could not bring myself to hold a conversation with them. So, I was not sure if any of these beautiful women that I was obsessing over were ever going to be the woman of my dreams. Honestly, I did not believe that any of these beautiful angels were the woman of my dreams. I did not believe that they were her because it was not her beauty that made her the woman of my dreams.

Beauty was not what made her the woman of my dreams since I was automatically assuming the woman of my dreams was beautiful. I was automatically assuming that she was beautiful because I learned to accept the fact that I will probably always be a shallow person. This acceptance of being shallow meant that I could not be with a woman unless she was beautiful. This did not mean that she had to be the most beautiful woman who ever existed. As a matter of fact, I did not want the supermodel type because I found them too intimidating to attain. Instead, I found that I was more attracted to the cute and angelic looking beautiful angels.

Beauty was what first attracted me to the beautiful blonde library angel. It was her beauty that kept me returning to the library. The time that I spent obsessing over her beauty at the library was what introduced me to my passion for writing. I never said anything to her. Thus, the only relationship I had with her was my imaginary relationship with her. This made me feel an emptiness to my relationship with her since it was never based upon reality. Even though it was never based upon anything real, I could still feel inspiration from her beauty. I could still feel this inspiration through my passion for writing. So, this was the power that beautiful women had over me during my spiritual journey, even though I had my social anxiety.

My beautiful blonde library angel introduced me to the power that a beautiful woman possessed. My beautiful blonde library angel also introduced me to the emptiness that went with only being obsessed over the beauty of a beautiful women. There was no denying the power of their beauty because for that brief moment when I saw them, I found an escape from the darkness. However, as great as I felt for that brief moment. Once that moment passed, the darkness always returned, and I remembered why I only had my obsession with them. This darkness is why the woman of my dreams must be more than a beautiful woman. I believe whoever this mysterious woman at my snowy log cabin is she must have other special qualities.

The mysterious woman of my dreams at the snowy log cabin had to have been very beautiful for me to leave my world of isolation and socialize with her. Therefore, I believe that her beauty is a given since I am such a shallow person. Yet, I also believe that there had to be some other qualities that made her the woman of my dreams as well. I believe that this woman of my dreams also had to be socially outgoing and compassionate. She must have been socially outgoing if she was able to break through my walls of fear and anxiety. Another special quality she must have possessed was that she must have also been compassionate. She must have been compassionate if she understood my debilitating social anxiety. I knew these were difficult qualities to find within a beautiful. Yet, I knew there were beautiful women with these qualities.

I knew there were beautiful women out there with these two qualities because I found them within a few of my objects of obsession. Annabelle was the first beautiful woman I met to have one of these qualities. Annabelle was someone who I was always socially comfortable around. Yet, the funny thing about her was that when I first met her, she was very shy because when we first met, she was hiding behind her parents. Then, we started spending all our time together as children. Finally, when I was to return to France, I still felt socially comfortable around her. Annabelle was my model for a beautiful woman I was socially comfortable around.

There were several other beautiful angels after Annabelle who had this quality of being socially outgoing. The beautiful blonde from high school who wrote me a letter because she was interested was definitely outgoing. So, I believe that she was socially outgoing as well. It was another few years before I met another woman who was also socially outgoing. The Mexican beauty was this other beautiful woman. Finally, there was this coworker that I was so socially comfortable around and I even developed a friendship with her. Yet, I never initiated a conversation with any of these beautiful women since my mind always went blank around them.

The initiator has to be confident. The initiator has to be very socially outgoing. The initiator has to be able to read the signs of women when they are interested. The initiator has to have the courage to approach beautiful women when he feels the signs are present. Thus, the initiator was never going to be me because I did not have any of these qualities. I was finding the confidence to start to develop some of these skills with my writing. However, I was only finding this confidence within my world of isolation. I was still not socially outgoing unless I felt socially comfortable around them first. The only way for this to happen was if they first initiated the conversation since another problem, I had was that I could not tell signs of interest.

I always had trouble telling the signs of beautiful women if they were interested. I believed that there might have been several opportunities for a romance if I could tell the signs. Sadly though, I never had a role model to teach me about these signs. One of these beautiful women might be giving me a sign as I am writing my book. There is this beautiful woman who could have decided to sit anywhere at the French Bistro since it was so empty there at the time. However, she decided to sit where I could see her, and I thought this might be a sign of interest. Sadly, I could not approach her because of my social anxiety. My social anxiety reminded me of the awkward silences that might happen if I approached her. So, I never approached her or tried to say anything to her. Instead, I wrote about how the woman of my dreams needed to be someone who could initiate a conversation with me if there was any hope for us getting together.

This chapter starts with me creating the vision I have of my snowy log cabin. This chapter continues with a look at how I will be spending my days at my snowy log cabin. I will be spending my days there with my passion for writing. My passion for writing will be the focus of the rest of this chapter because I believe this is how I will turn this dream into a reality. Maybe this dream will always remain a dream, however my pursuit of this dream will never die.

I believe the only way I will ever turn my dream of living at my snowy log cabin into reality is if I continue to cultivate my passion for writing and publish my books. This is what I believe because my inner strength derives from my passion for writing. I believe that we all have something within us that gives us our inner strength. For some of us, it might be playing a musical instrument. For some of us, it might be teaching. For some of us, it might be selling. For some of us, it might be socializing with people. For me, my passion for writing is what gives me my inner strength. Thus, if I had any hope of turning my dream of living at the snowy log cabin into a reality, I knew I had to turn to my passion for writing for this to happen. So, the question I had to ask myself was how could I turn the dream of my snowy log cabin into reality.

The only way that I was going to turn my dream into my reality was by writing. I was going to have to write a great deal for this to happen. It was my belief that the more I wrote, the more I was moving toward my dream of living at my snowy log cabin. So, every chance that I got, I was writing. As I started writing, I was also starting to think outside the box which was important because this was helping me find a solution to the limitations that I created for myself. One of these limitations was that I still felt as if I was unable to socialize with beautiful women or anyone else. I believed my fear of people was always going to exist. I believed this fear kept me feeling socially anxious. This social anxiety kept me searching for an escape from humanity whenever I had to socialize with them. I hated work because it meant I might have to socialize with people. I hated school because it meant I might have to socialize with my peers. Hence, I only felt comfortable when I was isolated and alone. My love for being isolated and alone was part of the appeal of the dream I had of moving to my snowy log cabin. When I imagined my snowy log cabin, the only other person there was the mysterious woman of my dreams. My snowy log cabin never included children, yet I was never against it if this was important to her.

I envisioned myself living at my snowy log cabin isolated and alone because I had accepted my social anxiety. I may not have liked this about myself. I may never be happy about not being able to feel socially comfortable around people. However, I learned from my time of going to therapy that you did not have to like something to accept it. Acceptance was more about redirecting my energy toward finding solutions while being well aware of my limitations. Acceptance was about finding a way of being content even if I was not happy. I felt it was important to find acceptance because it was helping me to get out of my life of misery. I started to accept that I was never going to be able to get a beautiful woman. My inability to get a beautiful woman was so depressing, that there were many days that I was unable to start my day.

The discovery of the beautiful blonde library angel changed all of this by giving me a reason to start my day. She was going to be giving me my reason to start my day by introducing me to my passion for writing. My passion for writing was great because it was my way of tolerating humanity. My social anxiety and my fear of humanity were never going to disappear. They were always going to exist because I was always going to have to deal with humanity. I had to deal with humanity at work since I could only tolerate customer service work. I could not tolerate factory work because I hated the heat more than I feared socializing with people. I had to deal with humanity when I was driving because of other drivers. Later, I learned that this fear I had of other drivers was the one good thing to derive from me not being a truck driver. I had to deal with humanity when I had to leave my locations of inspiration as well. Finally, I had to deal with humanity at home because my parents were also human beings. Thus, my social anxiety was never going to disappear since I could not escape my fear of humanity. Sadly, my depression was also something that did not disappear. My depression was never going to disappear either because as anxious as I felt socializing, I also felt the depression of being alone.

My love for beautiful women was equal to my fear of humanity. My love for seeing beautiful women was what kept me confronting my social anxiety. This same social anxiety was what kept me from talking to them. This social anxiety then led me to my depression. My feelings of anxiety and depression never did disappear, neither did my need to find some escape.

I found my escape with my world of isolation at my locations of inspiration. The beautiful blonde library angel was going to lead me to my first escape at the library. I was going to find my second escape at the French Bistro when I saw this beautiful super friendly angel. Then, another French Bistro was going to be my third escape since it had twice as many angels. Finally, this department store was my fourth escape during the Coronavirus because I was going to temporarily lose both French Bistros as my locations of inspiration. I was not sure how many locations of inspiration I was going to have during my spiritual journey. However, I felt as if I knew where my final location of inspiration was going to be located. I truly did believe that my final location of inspiration was going to be located at my snowy log cabin. I also believed the isolation of not being around other people meant that I did not need an escape while at my cabin.

I envisioned myself being isolated from humanity by the snow and the cold. I saw myself being isolated by the state of Alaska since it had the smallest population of other states. I found myself isolated there because of how far away I was from people. When I envisioned my snowy log cabin, I imagined the cabin being surrounded by forests and mountains. The nearest city or town was only about a half an hour away and I only went there for an emergency. Also, I wanted to be close to a town or city since the woman of my dreams wanted to socialize. I spend my days at this snowy log cabin pursuing my passion for writing. However, I believe if I am living at this snowy log cabin, I have already found success as a writer. Hence, I am only pursuing my passion for writing because it is something I want to do, not for any financial gain.

I envision myself as an accomplished writer at my snowy log cabin. I will have published enough books to afford to be isolated from humanity. However, I will continue my connection with humanity by my career as a writer and with the woman of my dreams. The woman of my dreams will continue to go to a nearby community because she wants to socialize.

My life at the snowy log cabin was the perfect world of isolation for me to escape to when I needed an escape from my socially anxious thoughts. My snowy log cabin might never turn into reality, yet it was always going to be a part of my spiritual journey. My vision of the snowy log cabin was my dream of the perfect future with the woman of my dreams. I hope someday this dream might be my reality. However, whether it turns into reality or it remains a dream, I knew it was going to continue to inspire my spiritual journey. My passion for writing was as important to my life as was my breath of life. My breath of life allowed me to live, however it was my passion for writing that was giving me a reason to get out of bed every day.

My passion for writing turned my snowy log cabin into more than a vision. It started during one of my meditations. It was during one of my meditations that I imagined this peaceful world of escape which was my snowy log cabin. As I spent more time envisioning my snowy log cabin, I was seeing myself sitting by the fireplace with the mysterious woman of my dreams. Once I started imagining us sitting by the fireplace at the snowy log cabin, I could not stop imagining this great escape. So, I started writing about it. The more I wrote about it, the more it started to have a life of its own. Then, I started to think about how to live every moment as a way of bringing myself closer to my snowy log cabin. The more I thought about how to turn my dream into a reality, the more I realized that my passion for writing was the key. I never could have envisioned my snowy log cabin without the beautiful blonde library angel. I will now introduce my two-and-a-half-year spiritual journey I took with the beautiful blonde library angel.

The Discovery Of My Beautiful Blonde Library Angel

The discovery of my beautiful blonde library angel changed my life forever. I first discovered my beautiful blonde library angel at the start of another hot summer. I always hated the heat because it made me so miserable and uncomfortable. I hated the heat because it made me feel as if I was trapped with no means of escape. My only means of escape from the heat was to go places where they had the air conditioner running. My parents had an air conditioner however they never ran it unless it was about a hundred degrees outside. This infuriated me so much because I was someone who was never able to tolerate a single minute of the heat. My intolerance for the heat was so great that I started a countdown for when the cold might eventually return. This countdown ran from March to October or May to October if I got lucky.

I could never understand how people could love the heat so much when it brought so many more people into the world. Bringing these people into the world congested the roads and made people angry because of all the traffic. Then, these angry people displayed their anger by passing people and cutting other drivers off. As I observed these angry people, I noticed one common theme. This common theme was the heat. The hotter it got; the more people went into the world. The more people that went into the world, the more the roads were congested. This led to more angry drivers and more people honking their loud horns which did not help. So, every time I heard people say they loved the heat, I could not understand why they loved something that made them so angry. All I knew was I hated the heat, and I needed an escape.

My search for an escape from the heat led me to the library. This library was only five minutes from my house. This library was something I always knew about; however, I never went there unless I had something to print because reading was not my favorite past time. However, all of this was about to change as I entered the library to escape the heat this Saturday.

I walked into the library to escape the heat and discovered the most beautiful blonde librarian I ever saw. My discovery of this beautiful blonde library angel changed my life forever.

I will never forget the first time I saw my beautiful blonde library angel. I will never forget what she was wearing or where she was standing. She was wearing a white T-Shirt and blue jeans. She was standing by the computers sorting through books and getting ready to put them away. This moment was a magical moment because it changed my life forever. This magical moment was the moment that led me to my rebirth and to creating my spiritual journey.

The first thing I think of when I think of this beautiful blonde library angel was her beautiful angelic face. It was because of her beautiful angelic face that I started to call her my beautiful blonde library angel. She had these beautiful brown eyes that blended wonderfully with her blondish brown golden hair. She had the cutest buttoned nose and a perfectly shaped mouth with the brightest white teeth. Finally, she had this amazing physique that I later learned was because she was an aspiring dancer. The first moment I saw this beautiful blonde library angel at the library I was mesmerized by her beauty and I placed her upon a pedestal. Unfortunately, this made her out of my league and had me believing that I could not talk to her.

I was only able to talk to my beautiful blonde library angel one time during my entire spiritual journey with her. The only time I was able to talk her was when I was feeling a sense of gratitude for everything I had within my life. I was feeling this sense of gratitude because of an article I read about being grateful for what you had within your life. This article had me thinking about all the things I was grateful for having within my life. I was feeling a sense of gratitude for my creative mind, my health, my parents, and finally I was feeling grateful for my senses. I was especially feeling this sense of gratitude for my sense of sight. How could I not feel this gratitude for my sense of sight when this was how I was able to see my beautiful angel. Feeling this sense of gratitude was inspiring me to write thank you notes. I wanted to write one to everyone who meant something special to my life, including my beautiful blonde library angel.

I wanted to thank her for being so beautiful. I wanted to tell her how her beauty was inspiring me to change my life. After hours of thinking about thanking her with a note, I finally found the confidence and courage to approach her and verbally thank her for being so beautiful. I blocked out and ignored all other thoughts as I approached her. Then I told her, "I simply had to tell you thank you for being so beautiful". Honestly, I do not remember my exact words to her. However, I know that I thanked her for being so beautiful. Then, she responded with an awkward giggle, and this was the only social interaction we shared with each other. This awkward giggle probably meant nothing to her, whereas I remember it as the giggle of an angel.

I still remember the exact moment when I saw her at the library. It was another hot Saturday. I was trying to think of where I could go to escape the heat. I could not stay home since my parents were not running the air conditioner. Yet, I also felt I had no right to say anything because it was not my house. I was a forty-one-year-old man who was still living at home with his parents, so I felt I had no right to say anything to them about anything. Also, I could not help them financially because it had been seven months since I was last employed. The last place that I worked at was at this refrigerated factory. This refrigerated factory was a great place to work for the most part. I enjoyed working with my coworkers, and I was getting great pay there. The problem was that I was getting so many hours there that it was leaving me no time for a life outside of work and this was making me hate my work there. This work was great if you had a family to support, however I did not have a family to support. So, I did not find the same value within making all this money as my other coworkers. It was also a good thing that I quit working there because I may not have discovered my passion for writing there.

It was May 2015 when I was hired to work at this refrigerated factory. I was looking forward to working there. I had two goals for working there. My first goal was to try and make as much money as possible to pursue my future as a truck driver. My second goal was to prove to BVR that I could keep this work. BVR was the name of the agency I was working with to help pay for truck driving school. It was an agency that helped those with disabilities find work. It was also called OOD (Opportunities for Ohioans with Disabilities). I had so much to prove when hired to work at the refrigerated factory. I had so much to prove because I walked out of the factory where I had previously worked. My decision to walk out of this factory could have cost me my future as a truck driver. I did not have much time to mourn the loss of my work at this factory, nor the loss of any chance I might have had with the Mexican beauty. I had to regroup and find work as soon as possible since my passion at the time was to be a truck driver.

I believed that the solution to the problem I had created was to find work as soon as possible. It took me about a week to find work again. I was determined to find some type of work before I was going to meet with my BVR counselor again. I found three places willing to hire me before I met with her. This was a relief, and I was hoping that once she saw my determination to find work so quickly, she was going to continue to help me with truck driving.

It was Saturday when I walked out of my work at this factory. I took about a day to enjoy my day off. I went to the movies and then I had a good dinner. Then Sunday, I was ready to start filling out applications and apply for work. Normally, once I lost my work, I started my search for work Monday and continued until Friday. Then, I took the weekends off before looking for work again. However, this time I could not wait to look for work because I knew there was a purpose to me working and saving money which was to be a truck driver. So, I started applying for work Sunday and this led me to having several interviews to go to Monday.

These interviews led me to having three choices for where to work when I saw my counselor. These choices for work also allowed me to focus more upon what was really making me depressed about losing my work at the factory when I went to see my counselor. When I finally met with my BVR counselor, I told her about leaving my work at the factory. I was very honest about my reasons for leaving my work at the factory. I always felt like my BVR Counselor was more my counselor than she was someone helping me find work. So, I felt it was important to be honest with her even if it might mean my future as a truck driver. I believe my being so honest and my resolve to finding work so quickly kept my dream of truck driving alive.

Another thing I spoke to my BVR counselor about was the loss of the Mexican beauty. This was the real loss when I walked out of my work at this factory. I did not care about the loss of my work at the factory because it was lousy pay under horrible working conditions. However, the loss of the Mexican beauty was something I was not sure how to handle. I knew I was going to eventually find work again and after finding this work my worry about finding work was over. However, the fear I had of never finding another beautiful angel who I was socially comfortable around was not something I was sure about ever finding again. Finally, after talking to my counselor for about two hours I convinced her that I was still very passionate about truck driving.

I had been working at this refrigerated factory for about seven months. I worked there from May to November. I had now saved enough money to quit and I was finally ready to start my future as a truck driver. Yet, I was having trouble deciding if I should quit or stay since I found this work so tolerable. Unfortunately, I knew I had to leave if I ever wanted to be a truck driver. So, I was at a crossroads, I had to choose between working at this refrigerated factory or my future as a truck driver. Honestly, the choice was not that difficult. I chose my future as a truck driver; however, I was not thrilled about leaving this factory because this was not a horrible place to work. I enjoyed my work at the refrigerated factory because it was so cold there. Another reason I did not want to leave was because of my coworkers there. I was so socially comfortable with all of them most of the time. I was going to miss the comradery of my coworkers. Also, I was making great money there because of all the hours we were working. Finally, I was going to miss the drives to work. It was during these drives through the country that I was starting to enter my world of isolation while listening to my music. The one thing I was not going to miss though was all the hours that we had to work there. I was not going to miss going to work at one and then wondering when it was that I was going to go home at night.

The worst part about working these hours was that much of this time we were not working. A great deal of this time at the factory was being spent sitting around waiting for the machines to work. Thus, I felt I was wasting away my life while working there. There were many times when I was waiting that I thought about simply driving off and never returning. However, I knew I had to stay to prove to BVR that I could keep my work. Finally, I found out the date for when I could leave work. October 31st, 2015 was going to be my last day at this refrigerated factory. I started counting down the days until I could start my life as a truck driver.

My last day at this refrigerated factory arrived. My future as a truck driver was a complete mystery when I left this factory. My path toward truck driving finally was going to start November 1st, 2015. I started my path as a truck driver by spending most of my time researching what it meant to be a truck driver. BVR wanted me to be sure that this was the future I wanted before they paid for school. So, I spent this time looking at schools and writing about my reasons for wanting to be a truck driver. I was doing most of my research at the library to escape the heat. Also, I was tired of being at home so much. Finally, once they were convinced, I wanted to be a truck driver, I was going to start to search for a truck driving school.

It was as I was doing research at the library that I started to cultivate my passion for writing. I was spending as much time journaling as I was doing research at the library. I spent five months doing research from November 2015 to March 2016. I spent my time doing this research at the library. Also, I was still meeting with my BVR Counselor hoping they were still going to pay for truck driving school. They really wanted me to think about my future as a truck driver because this was more than a career choice. It was going to be a change of lifestyle. Being a truck driver meant you were going to be driving a truck for several months at a time. This was going to be a life of great adventures. I was going to have the opportunity to travel across the country. This was very appealing because I had always loved to drive. Also, I loved the idea of getting paid to see the country. However, the life of a truck driver also had its drawbacks. You had to work fourteen-hour days, seven days a week. Also, truck driving meant spending most of your life alone. This was something that was both appealing and unappealing. I found it appealing since it was an escape from my social anxiety. I found it unappealing because I feared losing all hope of meeting someone. This loss of hope was a powerful feeling.

I chose to ignore this powerful feeling because I felt the benefits to truck driving were greater. I was more excited about the sense of adventure and getting to see the country. Also, I loved the idea of getting paid to drive. I have always had a passion for driving, although I learned that my passion for writing was greater when I lost my future as a truck driver. There were many doubts I chose to ignore as I was pursuing my future as a truck driver. There was the fear of safety that I felt after watching a video about keeping a gun under your seat for safety. Also, I never loved the idea of living the rugged life because of my OCD. I did not know how I was going to deal with having to take showers at gas stations. Also, I had to deal with not washing my hands. These were only some of the doubts that I was having before starting school.

I could not speak to my BVR counselor about many of these doubts because I feared it might lead to the loss of my dream of being a truck driver. I still felt my dream of being a truck driver was more powerful than my doubts were about being one. I felt the dream was more powerful because I was thinking of the joys of seeing the country. Also, I was thinking about how the truck was going to be my home away from home. I thought I finally found a way to move away from my parents. Unfortunately, when I think about these doubts today, I realize I should have been playing closer attention to them since they were telling me something. I believe these doubts were trying to tell me that truck driving was not the right path for my life.

I spent five months sorting through my fears and doubts about truck driving. I was convincing my counselor and myself that truck driving was the right path. Once we were both convinced that it was the right path, I started to look for a truck driving school. I started exploring which school to attend and I had a few interviews. Finally, I chose to go to this truck driving school that was close to where I was living. I started around March of 2016. I was finally going to start my path toward truck driving. I was very excited because I knew once I graduated, the school was going find me work right away. Thus, I believed that within a few months I was going to be driving a truck. The first few weeks of school were to be spent learning about the mechanics of a truck and the rules of the road. Then, started the real training.

The real training started when we started to learn the driving maneuvers and when we started driving the truck. The only important things we learned during class were reading maps and keeping logs of hours worked. Also, we met with recruiters during this class time to try to decide what company we wanted to work for when we graduated. I was feeling a great deal of social anxiety during class time because we spent a great deal of time socializing. I hated socializing with the other students because I was not comfortable with any of these people. All anyone was talking about were the relationships they had and other macho things. These conversations caused me to revert back to my invisible man complex during class. Thus, I was looking forward to getting out of class where I could finally start driving a truck. At the same time, I was also feeling very anxious because of all the stories I was hearing about driving trucks.

The last day of class arrived. It was time to start learning the driving maneuvers. This was when the real fear and anxiety started to develop since I had so much trouble learning them. My inability to learn the maneuvers made me feel very defeated because everyone else was able to learn the driving maneuvers without much effort. Then, there I was not even able to learn the simplest maneuvers. It took me about a week to learn how to back the truck within a straight line while everyone else was able to learn the maneuver their very first day. It took me about a week to learn this one maneuver. Then after learning it, it was time to move to some of the other driving maneuvers. We had several maneuvers we were going to have to learn for the exam, and I was not able to feel comfortable with any of the maneuvers. This was causing me so much anxiety that I did not know how I was going to pass the CDL Exam. However, I refused to quit.

I was going to keep trying until the school told me I could not continue anymore. I was at school every hour the instructors were available trying to learn the driving maneuvers. I tried everything I could think of to learn the driving maneuvers. I started to feel it was hopeless though because I was not able to feel comfortable with a single one of these driving maneuvers. Eventually, after several hours of practice, I was starting to learn some of the driving maneuvers. Yet, the one driving maneuver that I was not able to get comfortable with no matter how much I practiced was parallel parking. I was losing hope because I was running out of time. The school was only allowed so many hours of practice time by law and I was running out of hours. The time when I was not learning the driving maneuvers, I was studying the parts of a truck's engine.

There were four parts to passing the CDL exam. The first part of the exam involved identifying the ninety different parts of a truck's engine. The second part involved me learning the proper procedure for starting the truck's engine. The third part involved me learning the driving maneuvers. Finally, the last part of the exam involved me learning how to drive a truck.

I found I loved learning how to drive a truck. I also felt confident about this part of training because it was not as difficult as learning the maneuvers. This confidence was helping me learn the driving maneuvers as well. We spent about four hours a day learning the driving maneuvers, and then we were spending another four hours a day learning how to drive the truck.

I was feeling great about the driving portion of the exam. I was feeling confident about learning the parts of an engine. I was feeling confident about learning the right procedure to start the truck's engine for the exam. Sadly, the one thing I was still very concerned about was learning the driving maneuvers. Learning the driving maneuvers was stressing me out because no matter how much I practiced I was not getting parallel parking. This stress that I was feeling about passing the CDL exam was something I could not escape. However, I kept practicing the driving maneuvers believing that eventually I might learn them. I was not going to quit because I thought my future as a truck driver was my true life's passion. I believed that I was getting closer to learning the driving maneuvers. Then, there was parallel parking. This was the one maneuver I simply could not learn. I was getting very frustrated, plus I was running out of money. It had been seven months since I lost my work at this refrigerated factory, which meant my money was running dry and I had no way to replenish it. Both the financial stress of not making money and learning how to drive a truck were what led to the return of my migraines. The return of my migraines meant the loss of truck driving, and this was my escape from humanity. It was my loss of truck driving that was to lead me to my fall into my pit of darkness.

My Fall Into My Pit
Of Darkness

My fall into my pit of darkness started the moment my migraines returned because it meant the loss of my dream of being a truck driver. I had to let go of my dream of being a truck driver because I was unwilling take the chance of my migraines returning while driving a truck. It did not matter what my BVR counselor was going to say or what my school was going to say because once my migraines returned, I already decided that my dream was over. It was this decision to let go of my dream of driving a truck which caused me to fall into my pit of darkness.

I was relentless within my pursuit of driving a truck and passing the CDL exam before making this decision. I was relentless within my pursuit because I dreaded the idea of having to return to regular work. The idea of having to return to regular work meant that I was going to have to return to dealing with humanity and my social anxiety. Thus, I was relentless within my pursuit of truck driving because I saw it as my only escape from my debilitating social anxiety. I was studying at the library every night and then practicing the driving maneuvers every day. My passion for truck driving far outweighed the stress I felt about not passing the CDL exam. My philosophy while training to be a truck driver was to live within the moment. I refused to let the stress I was feeling for not passing my CDL exam stop me from enjoying the process of learning. I knew how much I loved learning how to drive a truck because of my passion for driving. I was even enjoying the process of learning the driving maneuvers. Unfortunately, the return of my migraines meant that I was going to have to let go my passion for driving and find a new passion.

I started this search for a new passion by going to the library to escape the heat of summer. I will never forget the day I walked into the library near my house to escape the heat because this was also the day when I was to first discover the beautiful blonde library angel. This discovery was so important because it was going to be what led to my passion for writing.

My obsession with her was unlike any obsession I had ever had before because it was never based upon anything real. My obsession with Annabelle was based upon "My Wonderful French Childhood" and her being one of my best friends. My obsession with the beautiful blonde from high school who wrote me a letter was based upon her being interested. My obsession with the Mexican beauty was based upon our time at the factory. The closest thing to my obsession with this beautiful blonde library angel was my obsession with celebrities. My obsession with celebrities was always solely based upon their looks. At times, it might have been based upon their voice, if they were singers, or their passion for life. This was the case for both Shania Twain and Jennifer Love Hewitt. Yet, my beautiful blonde library angel was not a celebrity. She was a real person working at the library. I believe this was part of the magic of this beautiful blonde library angel. I knew that with celebrities I never had any chance with them. This beautiful blonde library angel was not a celebrity though, she was someone working at the library right near my house. Her proximity to me had me imagining that despite her being so out of my league, I might have a chance with her one day. Granted, it may not have been much of a chance because of all the obstacles, such as our ages and my social anxiety.

Yet, it was a chance, and it was enough to give me hope and start my spiritual journey with her.

I lacked the confidence of ever having a chance with a beautiful woman when my spiritual journey started. I had accepted the sad reality of living my life alone and never knowing the warmth or love of a beautiful woman. I had accepted this as being my fate because of my debilitating social anxiety and my fear of humanity. Before my spiritual journey, I felt my fate was to live a meaningless life at home with my parents because I saw no hope for a better future. This lack of hope was why I fell into my pit of darkness. However, once I discovered the beautiful blonde library angel all of this changed. All of this changed because I was starting to imagine I had a chance with her, and this was giving me hope. It was not so much that I was feeling hopeful about attaining her, per say. It was more of someday attaining someone like her.

My beautiful blonde library angel was my symbol of hope. She had me believing that someday I might find the courage and confidence to approach someone like her. However, I was nowhere near finding this courage and confidence at the start of my spiritual journey. I knew I was going to need more courage and confidence before I could approach someone like her. Hence, I started to think of a way to find the confidence and courage I needed to approach them.

I was going to find this confidence and courage to talk to beautiful women with my passion for writing. My journey toward finding the courage and confidence to attain a beautiful woman started with the discovery of my beautiful blonde library angel. It started with her because she introduced me to my passion for writing. Once I was introduced to my passion for writing, I found I was starting to build my confidence through it. This confidence was helping me to start to think that one day I might be able to approach a beautiful woman like her. Eventually, I was even able to find the courage to approach a few of these beautiful women at my locations of inspiration. Granted, I was never successful when I approached them which made it difficult for me to find the courage to approach them again. However, through the pain of rejection I was also learning what worked and what did not work. The main thing I was learning was that I was going to have to find a way to gain the confidence to socialize with them.

I was unaware of the impact that my beautiful blonde library angel was going to have upon my life when I first discovered her. All I cared about when I first discovered her was her beauty. So, I went to the library every chance that I got to get a glimpse of this beautiful blonde librarian. Then, the more I went to the library to get a glimpse of her beauty, the more that I started to journal about her beauty. Gradually, my journaling turned into my passion for writing.

My passion for writing started with me finding a safe place to express myself. The library where the beautiful blonde library angel worked was going to be this safe place. The library was my new location of inspiration. I was at the library every chance I got after my beautiful blonde library angel introduced me to the power of my passion for writing. I did not need any money to develop my passion for writing. I only needed time to cultivate my writing. I found that the more time I had at the library the more confidence I was gaining. This confidence was leading me out of my pit of darkness and away from all my many dark thoughts.

Most of my thoughts were dark at the start of my spiritual journey. My thoughts were mostly about my fall into my pit of darkness. They were about the loss of truck driving and how I dreaded having to return to work. They were about my social anxiety and how I dreaded having to deal with having to socialize with people again. They were about how I saw my future as simply being a cycle of trying to work with people and failing over and over again. Finally, they were about how I saw my life as being meaningless and hopeless because I could not socialize with people. These thoughts were my reason for falling into my mental pit of darkness.

The CDL exam was about a week away when my migraines returned. Their return brought to a close my future as a truck driver. Yet, this future was still a possibility even after they returned if I could keep quiet about their return since I already passed the medical exam. Thus, I could have continued with training and never said a word to anyone. I had to say something though since I felt the risk was to great a risk to take. So, I decided to say something.

My migraines were my handicap much like my social anxiety. The scariest thing about my migraines is that they will happen out of the blue and without warning. I might be at work or driving when all of a sudden, I will get a migraine. These migraines mean I will be unable to function visually and mentally for about two hours of my life. The terrifying mental process will start with me being nearly blind for about a half an hour. For this half hour, my vision will be obstructed, and I will be rendered functionless. Then after waiting the half hour, I will try to start functioning normally again since my vision will have returned. However, even when my vision returns, I will not be back to functioning normally. Once my vision returns, I will spend another hour and a half feeling the aftereffects of my migraine. I will feel a lingering headache and confusion, so the entire process of my migraines will take about two hours to completely run its course. I saw several doctors about my migraines. Unfortunately, they never were able to do anything to help. So, I had to learn to live life at the mercy of my migraines. These migraines went dormant for a few months before reappearing. This is what happened before truck driving.

I was a week away from taking my CDL exam. This was when I fell into my pit of darkness. I do not remember what I was doing when my migraines returned. All I remember is that when they returned, it meant my future as a truck driver was over. After losing my future with truck driving, I was feeling anxious and depressed as I thought about how to move forward. I did not want to return to a life of doing regular work. Thus, when I think back to the loss of truck driving, this was not what led me to my pit of darkness. I fell into my pit of darkness because the loss of truck driving meant my return to my social anxiety and my fear of humanity.

I was not too sad about the loss of truck driving because I did not believe that truck driving was the right path for my life. I had too many doubts and too much stress about truck driving for this to be the right path for me to follow. I think that subconsciously, I knew this at the time. However, I was not willing to let go of truck driving because I dreaded returning to work way too much. Then once my migraines returned after being dormant for two years, I saw them as a sign from my body to let go of my dream of being a truck driver. Before the CDL exam, the stress of being broke and passing the exam was overwhelming. Yet, I kept practicing and I kept studying at the library because I wanted my escape from humanity. Then, my migraines returned, and I knew it was over. I knew my body was trying to tell me something.

"Stop pursuing a future as a truck driver!" These were the screams that I was hearing when my migraines returned. I could not ignore these screams anymore. I knew it was time to start the process of letting go of my future of being a truck driver. I first started the process of letting go by letting the truck driving school know I had to quit my training. Once I let the truck driving school know, I was asked how I got through the medical exam with my migraines. I told them my migraines had been dormant for about two years, so I was hoping they had disappeared. The school was willing to let me take a leave of absence as I tried to get treatment for my migraines. However, I knew there was no treatment for my migraines. I knew my future as a truck driver was over for the rest of my life once my migraines returned. After letting the school know, I had to let my BVR counselor know about my dream of being a truck driver being over. When I went to let BVR know, I was expecting support and financial assistance as we searched for a new path to follow. However, this was not the way my meeting with them went at all. Instead, once I told them about my migraines, they told me their services with me were also over.

These were both two very devastating losses for me to have to deal with at the time. It took me some time to recuperate from both of these losses. I spent two years of my life training and preparing for a future as a truck driver. I spent two years looking forward to escaping humanity and my social anxiety. Thus, I was truly devastated when I lost my dream of being a truck driver. However, as devastated as I was about the loss of truck driving, I still felt very confident that I made the right decision by telling them about the return of my migraines. I felt this was the right decision because I did not want to gamble with my life to be a truck driver. Nonetheless, I was still devastated over the loss of truck driving, so I fell into my pit of darkness.

I dreaded the idea of spending the rest of my life working at some factory or some call center. I believed my return to doing regular work was a return to feeling as if I was going to be trapped within a dark existence that I could not escape. I felt the only escape from this dark existence was death, so I was not willing to enter this life of misery. Instead of living this life, I was starting to find an escape from reality at the library. I had no money when I fell into my pit of darkness. So, the library was the only place I could go to escape my reality. So, my fall into my pit of darkness was more about returning to work than the loss of truck driving. I simply could not bring myself to go through the motions of applying for work again. I could not imagine returning to regular work when I thought I finally found my escape with truck driving.

I imagined myself driving across country having these great adventures while also making money. I did not know what to expect from this life as a truck driver. Yet, I was very excited by the idea of driving a truck and seeing the country. Unfortunately, my migraines returning meant the loss of truck driving and it meant my return to having to do regular work.

I knew finding employment was going to be the first step toward creating a future for myself. I knew I had to work because I knew I had to make money. At the start of my spiritual journey, I simply did not see any other way to make money other than regular work. The problem with regular work was that I could not find the motivation to apply for work. Therefore, applying for work was going to be the second step for me to move forward. The actual first step involved me searching within myself for the motivation to return to regular work. I knew I needed money. The problem was that the necessity of money was not enough of a motivation. I knew I needed money for survival. However, it did not matter how much I needed money to survive because it was not enough of a reason to work. This led to a great deal of soul searching.

I started my search for this motivation to return to work by first realizing that making money was not the most important thing to my life. I knew I was always going to need money to survive. I knew that I was going to need money to eat, for an internet connection, to keep my car, and to get Pepsi. The need for money was never going to disappear because like it or not you needed money to survive. Thus, I needed to find some way to get the motivation to return to work. However, this was not a simple thing for me to do because I knew how much I dreaded to work. This was the true reason of why I fell into my pit of darkness. I fell into my pit of darkness because I knew I had to return to work which was a very difficult thing for me to accept because I was not motivated to return to work at all, and when I say at all I mean at all. I was sitting at the library thinking of filling out an application and I could not see the point if I was simply going to start work and walk out about a week later. I could not see myself keeping employment even if I was offered employment. Thus, I fell into a literal mental pit of darkness.

My fall into my pit of darkness was about my lack of motivation to work. It was not about my lack of motivation to live my life. It was about me trying to figure out a way to make money doing something I dreaded five days a week. My lack of motivation was not even about finding work because I could find the motivation to fill out the applications. It was more about finding the motivation to do the work once hired. This was a very difficult thing for me to do after a lifetime of dreading work. I always dreaded working so my lack of motivation to work was not new territory. Whenever I found myself out of work before, I could always move past my unwillingness to work by applying for some other employment. The problem was that once I found this other employment, I was never able to remain at work after being hired. Thus, I was always going from one employer to another never able to stay at one place for much time. However, I continued to apply for work because I knew that no matter how much I hated to work I also always needed to make money. This cycle of work continued until I thought I found an escape with truck driving. Then, my migraines were to return, and I fell into my pit of darkness.

My fall into my pit of darkness led me to a time of reevaluating my life. I had to think about how I was going to move forward after the loss of truck driving. I knew eventually I was going to be able to find a way to work again. However, I also knew about my history of not keeping work because of my lack of motivation. Also, my social anxiety was not helping at all.

I was working at a call center before I started to pursue my future as a truck driver. I found this work at this call center very challenging because of my social anxiety. Yet, I found a way to keep this work for about a year before finally getting fired. I kept this work by hanging up on people when my social anxiety got too uncomfortable which was almost every call. Once I was fired, I started to believe that I was unable to work regular work anymore. I believed that my social anxiety was too powerful for me to ever find a way to do regular work again. I believed this because of my time at the call center. My work at a call center started off as work that I was very serious about keeping. I was motivated to keep this work because I was hoping it might help me learn some social skills. My work there started out great during training. I was one of the top students there. I even made an appointment with the owner of the call center to talk about how to succeed at work with my social anxiety. After this meeting, I had great aspirations about working at this call center. Sadly, these aspirations disappeared after training.

My social anxiety was overwhelming when I started taking calls. I dreaded going to work every day while at the call center. However, I was able to find a way to get through each day for about a year while working there. My main motivation for wanting to stay at this call center was because I was so focused upon my goal of returning to Alaska. I had this goal of returning to Alaska after three months of living there because of its beauty. Also, there was my love for the cold. I had a plan to save about $25,000, then I was going to move to Alaska. Unfortunately, my social anxiety was much more powerful than my dream of moving to Alaska.

My social anxiety was going to lead me to getting fired from this call center. I was able to remain at the call center for about a year. However, once my social anxiety started to be more powerful than my dream of moving to Alaska, I started to self-sabotage myself at work. I started to self-sabotage myself at work by calling off work and hanging up on customers. I was self-sabotaging myself at work because my social anxiety was making me so uncomfortable. So, I knew once I started hanging up on customers it was only a matter of time before I got fired. I knew that call centers were not going to tolerate me being rude to customers. However, I did not care because once I found an escape from my social anxiety there was no going back. Even though, I knew I was eventually going to get fired I was not willing to quit. It only took them about two weeks to find out I was hanging up on customers and to finally tell me that I was fired.

I felt an overwhelming amount of anxiety after getting fired from this call center. My anxiety made it difficult for me to find work. This overwhelming anxiety about not being sure how I was going to find work led me to truck driving. I saw truck driving as my escape from having to do regular work. I could not see myself doing regular work anymore when I knew what it involved. I could not see myself working at a call center again because I could not deal with the social anxiety of talking to people so much. I knew I did not want to work at a factory because of the heat. I could not work at a fast-food restaurant since this was a combination of dealing with people, the heat, the grease, and it was for lesser pay. Lastly, I could not do retail work since it meant interacting with people without the barriers of phones. I simply could not see any work I could tolerate after this call center. However, I knew I still needed money. Hence, this was when I turned to truck driving and its loss led to my fall into my pit of darkness.

My Beacon Of Hope

My beautiful blonde library angel was my beacon of hope after falling into my pit of darkness. I lost all hope of ever having a better future after my migraines returned, and I lost my dream of being a truck driver. This dream of being a truck driver was all I thought of for two years of my life. I was not sure how I was going to return to regular work again because I still remembered the anxiety, that I felt from the call center I was working at before truck driving. It was my social anxiety that led me to truck driving since working at a call center was the only work, I thought I could tolerate. After I returned from Alaska, I knew my dream of being a counselor was over. What I found more devastating than this loss though was the loss of Alaska.

I was devastated by the loss of Alaska because Anchorage, Alaska was one of the most beautiful places I had ever been. I remember walking out of my room and any direction I looked I was seeing beautiful mountains within the background. Another thing I remember about Alaska was that after about five minutes of leaving my room I was walking through a forest. It did not matter where I went there was always a beautiful, peaceful forest for me to walk through. Then, there was the reason why I chose The University of Alaska within the first place, the cold weather. Finally, it did not hurt that I saw some of the most beautiful women I had ever seen during my four months move to Alaska. There were beautiful women from Russia, Hawaii, Alaska, and one from Texas. I could not think of a better place to live than Anchorage, Alaska.

I learned that I had to leave Alaska after four months for two reasons. The first reason why I had to leave was for plagiarizing a paper for one of my classes. The second reason why I had to leave was because I took one too many classes. This led me to having to leave Alaska because I ran out of money. After talking to an administrator, I learned that I was getting suspended for a year for plagiarizing. So, I had an opportunity to return to The University of Alaska if I wanted to continue my path as a counselor and these were my plans. Then right before I left, one of my professors told me how my counseling skills needed a great deal of work.

I always had my doubts about wanting to be a counselor. I always had these doubts because of my social anxiety. The support I was getting from Portage Path helped me to ignore these doubts though, so I continued to pursue my dream of being a counselor. Also, I was going to the Psychology lab every day to cultivate my passion for writing. This was when I started to discover my world of isolation and the power of my passion for writing. I discovered the power of my passion for writing as I saw how my essays were getting me into graduate school. However, this was only a taste of how powerful my passion for writing could be if I took the time to cultivate it. It was not until I lost my world of isolation as I was pursuing my dream of being a counselor and found it again after I lost truck driving that I found its true strength. However, before this could happen, I had to start to explore other paths to find my true passion.

I started to develop my dream of being a counselor during high school while skipping school. I was spending most of my time at bookstores reading books while skipping school. I started out only reading autobiographies by people I found inspirational. I read autobiographies by John Travolta, Napoleon, Jennifer Love Hewitt, Shania Twain, and William Wallace. I found each of these individuals were inspirational for different reasons. John Travolta was someone I found inspirational because he was making his acting comeback at the time. He was nominated for an Oscar for Pulp Fiction and had hit after hit after having disappeared for about ten years. Napoleon inspired me because of his size and how he was overlooked as a child, not because he was a tyrant. Also, there was the fact that Napoleon was French. I found Jennifer Love Hewitt inspirational because she had such a cheerful personality. Shania Twain was inspirational because she had a drive to pursue her passion even after her parents died. It also did not hurt that Jennifer Love Hewitt and Shania Twain were so beautiful. Finally, William Wallace was inspirational because of Braveheart. Braveheart was my favorite movie of all time. I must have watched it about twenty-five times during high school. The speeches, scenery, music, and history were very inspirational. This may have been part of the reason why I joined the military.

I was reading these autobiographies because I loved learning about the psychology of these famous celebrities and historical figures. I loved learning what inspired them to confront their challenges. Their inspirational stories were helping me feel inspired to confront my own challenges. The only problem I had with reading these stories was that I did not feel I could relate to these individuals because none of them were dealing with social anxiety. John Travolta, Napoleon, Jennifer Love Hewitt, Shania Twain, and William Wallace were all extroverted. At least, I believed they were socially outgoing people. So, as inspirational as I found their stories, they were not helping me to develop a road map to confronting my social anxiety. I had to search elsewhere for this road map. My search was going to lead me to reading self-help books.

My locations of inspiration were going to be bookstores. I did not need any money to read books and these bookstores were my escape from the heat. I was also going to bookstores because I was able to see some beautiful women studying there. So, I started out reading autobiographies, then I turned to self-help books for ways to confront my social anxiety. I thought reading these self-help books were going to magically make my social anxiety disappear. Unfortunately, this never happened because once I was done reading and I left my world of isolation I had to return to my dark reality. This return to reality meant a return to not being able to socialize with beautiful women. Self-help books were inspiring me to want to change though by helping me to learn more about myself and my social anxiety. The more I learned about myself and my social anxiety, the more I started thinking about my past. This knowledge was a way for me to learn how to accept myself and find ways to move forward. Finally, this knowledge was starting to awaken one of my first passions, this was my passion for Psychology.

This passion for psychology followed me to Ohio. It also led me to Portage Path and therapy. Therapy was the only place that I felt safe enough to express myself before I found my passion for writing. My therapists were helping me learn more about myself. One thing I was learning about myself was my love for knowledge. My love for knowledge as well as the support of my therapist is what led me back to college. At first, I chose French as my major. However, after my doubts about finding work as a French Major, I switched to Psychology. Switching to Psychology and my time with my therapists led to my dream of being a counselor. I chose to pursue my dream of being a counselor despite my doubts. These doubts derived mostly from my social anxiety. Finally, I got a bachelor's degree and made the move to Alaska.

This was the fifth time I tried unsuccessfully to move away from my parents. I really wanted this move to Alaska to be a success. However, this was another failed attempt at moving out. I was never successful at moving out because of my social anxiety. I was never able to develop the social skills needed to meet new people. This led me to start self-sabotaging myself after moving out every time. I started to accept that moving away from my parents was never going to happen after returning from Alaska. I was also starting to accept my social anxiety. Accepting my social anxiety, meant I had to start to think about a new path to follow. I was thinking that the answer might be either accounting or truck driving. I thought both these choices were good for my social anxiety. However, I thought of truck driving as being the better choice because of my passion for driving. I could not think of a better way to make a living than to drive a truck all day. I imagined these great adventures as a truck driver and saw it as my escape from having to socialize with people and doing regular work. Even though I was starting to think my new path might be truck driving, I was not ready to pursue it quite yet. So, I returned to regular work for another three years. I worked at a retail store and two call centers.

My work at this second call center was what finally led to my dream of being a truck driver. I believed I was never going to be able to do regular work because of my social anxiety. So, I was finally ready to see if it was possible for me to pursue my dream of being a truck driver. I pursued my dream of being a truck driver for about two years before falling into my pit of darkness. This journey started with me talking to my therapist about being a truck driver. Then with my therapist's support, I got the financial support I needed from BVR to start my dream of being a truck driver. I worked at the factory with my Mexican angel and the refrigerated factory. Then, this led to truck driving school and my fall into my pit of darkness.

My only escape from my pit of darkness was the beautiful blonde library angel as she introduced me to my passion for writing. I believed that my passion for writing was going to be my way of telling the world about the power of my obsession with beautiful women. I had to show the world that being obsessed with beautiful women did not have to be this negative thing. I wanted to show the world how it could also be a source of creative strength. Yes, I may have never said anything to this beautiful blonde library angel. Yet, she was still someone special because she was this writing muse who was still inspiring my passion for writing. Do not get me wrong, I still wish I had been able to say something to her. However, I did not believe that this was something I was ever going to be able to do because of my debilitating social anxiety. This brings me to the real reason why I wanted to write this book. The real reason why I wanted to write my book was to give a voice to the voiceless. I wanted to write my book for anyone who was suffering from social anxiety so much that they could not find the courage to socialize. Sadly, I knew too much about this since my social anxiety was why I was a man without a voice.

The written word was the only way that I knew how to express myself. My world of isolation was the only place I felt safe enough to express my most vulnerable thoughts. I never could have found the safety of my world of isolation without my beautiful blonde library angel. My obsession with this beautiful blonde library angel was what kept me at the library. The more time I spent obsessing over her, the more time I spent journaling about her inspirational beauty. Eventually,

I was ready to make a powerful choice to see where this obsession with her might lead. Making this powerful choice was the turning point of my life. This was when I was reborn to start my spiritual journey with her. This was the moment I stopped hiding from my obsessions with beautiful women and I started to feel the creative and spiritual energy of these obsessions. My beautiful blonde library angel gave me a reason to live again by introducing me to my passion for writing. My obsession and my passion for writing led me out of my pit of darkness.

My spiritual journey started out being about my unwillingness to return to regular work. I saw regular work as being nothing more than extroverted work where I had to socialize with people. I was unwilling to apply for this work because I felt my social anxiety had me defeated after working at the last call center I had worked at before my venture into truck driving. I was not only unwilling to do this work, I felt I was unable to do this work as well. So, I started to think outside the box to other ways of making money. I started watching videos of how others suffering from social anxiety were making money. Then, I started looking into how to be a freelance writer. Mostly, I was spending my time at the library doing a great deal of journaling.

Journaling was the vehicle leading me out of my pit of darkness. I found no greater joy than journaling at the library within the presence of my beautiful blonde library angel. The more I journaled within her presence, the better I was feeling. The more I listened to my music as I was journaling within her presence, the better I was feeling. The more time I was spending at the library listening to my music within her presence and it was cold, the better I was feeling. Finally, the more I journaled within her presence listening to music with the cold and the sweet taste of my Pepsi, the better I was feeling. Ultimately, I never felt better than when all five of these elements converged. It was the convergence of all five of these elements at the library that led me to discovering the magic of the library. The magic of the library was first felt after discovering my beautiful blonde library angel. So, I was always at the library if she was present.

The rediscovery of my world of isolation led me to realizing my values. I realized that time was my most valuable resource. Time was my most valuable resource since this was how I was able to cultivate my passion for writing. I knew this passion for writing always existed because I always had this dream of writing a book. I never had the confidence to follow this dream though until I had this moment of clarity at the library. I had this moment of clarity when I remembered my dream of writing a book. I was reborn after this moment of clarity and my spiritual journey officially started. At the start of my journey, the path was not very clear though since I knew no one else who was pursuing a life as a writer. Hence, my spiritual journey of being a writer involved me following my gut instincts and they told me to follow my obsessions.

My spiritual journey started with me splitting my time at the library. I spent part of my time at the library doing research into ways of making money from the computer. I spent part of my time journaling. I spent part of my time making plans for how to start my spiritual journey. Mostly, I spent my time at the library writing a book about my life. I found this time spent writing was very therapeutic and it was giving my life some purpose. I knew this passion I had for my writing was going to be the fuel I needed to escape my pit of darkness. I knew that no matter what happened from this point forward, I was always going to have my passion for writing. I was not sure if I was ever going to find a way to make any money from it. However, I knew that unless I was to lose my hands or vision, I was always going to write. Once I was introduced to my passion for writing, I was excited to see where this new path was going to lead.

There was one more piece of the puzzle to my moment of clarity before I was ready to escape my pit of darkness. This last piece of the puzzle was going to be my depression support group which I go to every Tuesday. During this depression support group, we were going to explore our values. I was not paying much attention during this group since I was bored and uncomfortable. However, after group I spent the rest of the day looking at the handouts and I thought about my values. The more I thought about my values, the more I realized how my values were different from the rest of society. Most of society valued money, family, socializing, and work. I valued my passion for writing, my passion for music, my obsession for beautiful women, and finding the time to watch television. This led me to realize that what I valued most of all was time because without time none of these things were going to be possible.

I started to think about how to find more time to pursue my values by gaining the confidence to ignore the values of other people. I was not going to let society determine how I was going to spend my time anymore. My values and how I was going to make time for them was going to be the first thing that I was going to explore with my passion for writing. Thus, this support group was an important step toward my passion for writing. It was an important step since it inspired my passion for writing. As I started to explore my values, I was uncovering the elements that were creating my world of isolation. These elements were my Pepsi, my passion for writing and music, the cold, and the beautiful blonde library angel. These elements converged to create my world of isolation which is where I went to start to cultivate my writing.

I had my moment of clarity after returning from this support group. My moment of clarity appeared while I was walking into the library after group. I went to the library for another day of journaling except this time I felt I was ready to do more than journal. This time I was ready to start writing a book. This thought of writing a book was my moment of clarity because it had me thinking what did I have to lose by pursuing my dream of writing a book. I had no family to support. I had no girlfriend. I had no friends. I had no money. So, I had nothing to lose by writing a book. So, from this point forward my time at the library went from me simply going there to see my beautiful blonde library angel to me going there to write my book. My obsession with her continued though since it was what I wrote about for the most part. So, this moment of clarity was also when this beautiful blonde from the library was to turn into my beautiful blonde library angel. I was now ready to create some new plans to follow at the library.

The first step of my spiritual journey started with me making plans for how to move forward. My path started with me thinking about ways to best split my time at the library. My way of splitting my time at the library alternated according to what worked best. At first, my time at the library was split four ways. I was spending the first part of my day at the library making plans for how to find time to get to everything. I spent the second part of the day journaling. I spent the third part of the day researching freelance writing. Finally, I spent the rest of the day pursuing my passion for writing. I was now starting to feel as if I was going to the library for a purpose. I was going to the library to pursue my passion for writing. I was also starting to learn that this first way of splitting my time was not working. This first way of me splitting my time was not working because I was too overwhelmed by my research about freelance writing. I felt my time was better spent cultivating my passion for writing. Thus, I let go of my pursuit of freelance writing. Yet, I knew that this was always something that I could return to later once I was a writer. Once I made my plans for how to best split my time at the library, I felt my spiritual journey was finally falling into place. So, started my spiritual journey.

My passion for writing led to my internal rebirth since it gave my life purpose and meaning. Writing was all that I wanted to do with the rest of my life. I started spending hours after hours at the library pursuing my passion for writing. I did not care about anything else other than my beautiful blonde library angel and my passions for music and writing. Add to this my love for the cold and the sweetness of my Pepsi and I found where I was happiest. The more time I spent pursuing my passion for writing, the less I found myself wasting time at the library. Eventually, my ways of spending my time at the library evolved once more. My time spent making plans turned into me spending only five minutes a day looking them over. Then Saturdays, I was spending about two hours creating a table for my plans for the rest of the week.

Journaling was still important because it was my time for unstructured writing. I was also creating some power point presentations for my positive affirmations. I was hoping that if I started reading these presentations to myself my confidence might improve. I was also hoping that this might subconsciously help to change my way of thinking. Finally, I was also starting to apply for work again. This time I spent applying for work was replacing all the time I had been spending looking into ways to make money from my computer since I was feeling more confident about returning to work. I felt more confident because I found my passion for writing.

My passion for writing helped me to find this confidence by giving my life purpose outside of me returning to work. I stopped seeing work as something I had to do for the rest of my life. Do not get me wrong I still dreaded going to work every day, however now when I suffered through my workdays, I believed they were mere steppingstones to my being a writer. I was now spending every minute I was not at work at the library pursuing my passion for writing. Also, I went to the library every chance I got to see my beautiful blonde library angel. So, my beautiful blonde library angel led me out of my pit My Five Beautiful Library Angels

My five beautiful library angels consisted of the beautiful blonde library angel and four other beautiful library angels who worked there. These four other library angels were substitutes for those times when the beautiful blonde library angel was not working at the library. So, my beautiful blonde library angel was not the only beautiful angel inspiring my spiritual journey. I could not get enough of seeing these beautiful angels at the library every day. I felt each one of these angels were inspiring me to move forward and find a way out of my pit of darkness. Yet, my beautiful blonde library angel was always the most special of all these library angels. Unfortunately, she was not always at the library. Hence, there were times I needed a substitute.

My discovery of these four library angels was another turning point during my spiritual journey because it led me to spending even more time at the library. The more time I spent at the library, the more time I had to cultivate my passion for writing. The library was the only place I felt comfortable enough to cultivate my passion for writing. It was the only place I could go where all five elements of my world of isolation converged. Again, these five elements were my passion for writing, my passion for music, Pepsi, the cold, and my beautiful angels. I created this world of isolation when I wore my headphones and I started to listen to my passion for music. Whenever I started to listen to my music, I was able to block out humanity. Once I blocked out humanity, I started to express my most personal and vulnerable thoughts through my writing. Then, if I had a Pepsi and it was cold the comfort level increased even more. Finally, discovering these five beautiful library angels made this world of isolation a place I never wanted to leave. I was going to spend two-and-a-half-years obsessing over these five beautiful library angels. It was during this time at the library that I was creating my spiritual journey. So, these five beautiful library angels were the most important part of my life for about two-and-a-half-years.

My beautiful blonde library angel was the first of my five beautiful library angels that I went to see at the library. I will never forget my beautiful blonde library angel since she was the one who started it all. About a year passed since I last saw her at the library, yet I still feel her spiritual energy whenever I am reminded of her beauty. Two things reminded me of her beauty.

The first thing to remind me of her beauty was when I took a break from my passion for writing to get a Pepsi from a nearby department store. I entered Control and this was when I saw my beautiful blonde library angel. I could not miss her when I saw her there because she was walking right before me with her bright white smile. I could not have timed it more perfectly, even if I tried. There she was wearing her scarlet red lipstick and smiling at me with her bright white teeth. She was wearing a pair of blue jeans and a green sweater. I could not believe my eyes when I saw her, and it took a few second for me to realize it was her. Then, when I realized it was her, I was staring at her for a few more seconds since I could not believe it was her. After I recognized that it was her, I was feeling anxious and confused. I was feeling anxious and confused because her boyfriend was standing there waiting for her and I wanted to see her again.

I tried to act as normal as I could after I saw her at Control. I went to get a Pepsi after seeing her. Then, I tried my best to go for my walk around the store to see what other beautiful angels were at Control. However, I could not stop looking for her, so I chose to go wash my hands before my walk around the store instead, because she went to the restroom after I saw her. So, I was hoping to see her after I washed my hands. Thus, after getting my Pepsi, I went to wash my hands instead of going for my walk around the store. I was feeling scared and anxious when I went to wash my hands though since her boyfriend was standing there waiting for her. This fear and anxiety did not stop me though because I had to see my angel one more time. After washing my hands, I saw her watch dog still standing there and I knew she had not left yet.

I started to go for my walk around Control after washing my hands because I was still hoping to get one more look at my angel. Then, I decided to leave Control since I knew nothing could top seeing her there that one time. Then, I realized a year had passed since I got my last glimpse of my beautiful blonde library angel. So, I wanted to write about seeing my angel again.

I was not sure if I was going to be able to feel her spiritual energy once I got to the French Bistro since I was feeling confused by what seeing her meant. She had a boyfriend who I felt was very intimidating since he was standing there waiting for her with his arms crossed. It was as if he was her own personal security guard or watch dog. This reminded me of my time of being bullied during elementary school and middle school, so I felt very uncomfortable. I was confused though because I also had an urge to see her again at Control. However, I knew I was not going to say anything to her if I saw her, so all I was going to do was look at her. I feared this might lead to her boyfriend approaching me or even worse ruin that moment when I saw her.

These were the thoughts going through my mind when I left Control and returned to the French Bistro. I tried to feel her spiritual energy with my passion for writing when I got back to the French Bistro. However, when I first got there, I was too distracted by how warm it was, and I was constantly turning my head to see her if she left because my back was to Control. So, I decided to move to where I might see her green shirt leaving within the distance. Also, I went to wash my hands and face to cool off. So, I found a better place to sit and I was feeling more comfortable after washing my hands and face. Plus, I had gotten out my mini fan that I carried with me for these such occasions when it was too warm. Unfortunately, I never did see her green shirt again within the distance. Thus, I only saw her that one time at Control. However, I was able to feel her spiritual energy again once I got more comfortable. I was able to feel her spiritual energy again with the support of both my passion for writing and my passion for music.

"My beautiful blonde library angel resides where angels sing!" This is what still resonates with me after writing about my real dream with my beautiful blonde library angel. This real dream was not the first real dream I had of her, however it was one of the most powerful real dreams I had of her because I had it before I ever even saw her at Control again.

This real dream started out with her running through a drive thru movie theater. She wore red lipstick and other make up that made it look as if she never cracked a sweat. She was wearing this beautiful prom dress that might have been red or green, I am not quite sure. She was running through the movie theater chasing after someone. For the purposes of my dream, I started to imagine she was chasing after me because she found out that I wrote a book about her. Finally, she found someone with a motorcycle and tried to convince them to let her borrow it. After, she was unsuccessful at getting it, she stole the bike and continued the chase. Then, she road off the road and fell off the bike. This led to everyone laughing at her. This did not bother her though because I always believed her to be a very confident person. This was another wonderful quality I loved about her. After she continued the chase, I awoke from the real dream.

I spend the entire day thinking about my real dreams after I have them. I am usually spending the day thinking about their meaning because all I remember from them is a short clip. So, I will start off my day trying to remember the short clip from my real dreams. Then, I will spend the rest of my day thinking about why I was dreaming about this short clip. Thus, as I started writing about this real dream, my passion for music was going to be very important. It was important because it set the mood for me to write about this real dream. Meatloaf's "Welcome To the Neighborhood" was my album of choice for this real dream. This album was my album of choice because I felt this music could be playing at a drive thru movie theater. Mostly, this was because the album cover looked like something from a drive thru movie theater.

This Meatloaf album was a powerful album to listen to while writing about my real dream with her. The last song of the album was "Where angels Sing" and this song was the most powerful song of the album. One reason why this song was so powerful was because of the guitar solos from this Meatloaf song. Some of my favorite songs have some of the most powerful guitar solos I ever heard. One song that stands out as having the best guitar solo, I ever heard is Kitaro's Kokoro. It has a guitar solo that lasts about seven minutes. This meatloaf song also has a powerful guitar solo, although it lasts nowhere near seven minutes. This powerful guitar solo only lasts about a minute and is played twice during the song. What makes it such a powerful guitar solo though is the lyrics that are sung between the two solos. The best line from these lyrics is "where a good man just gets stronger". So, there I was listening to the Meatloaf song over and over again while staring at this beautiful image of her. As I listened to this powerful and inspirational song and I was looking at her image, I felt her spiritual energy return.

I was trying to figure out what made this beautiful blonde library angel so special as I was feeling her spiritual energy while listening to this Meatloaf song. It had been a year since I last saw her working at the library. Yet, I still felt her powerful spiritual presence. I felt this spiritual presence when I was cultivating my writing within my world of isolation. I also felt it when listening to a powerful inspirational song. I knew her beauty and her timing made her special. However, there was more to her than even that which made her special. Another thing that made her so special was that we never spoke to each other and I never tried to approach her. Thus, I was never rejected by her or hurt by her. This is what allowed me to think of her as my beautiful perfect angel who only appeared to me within my world of isolation. Then, as I was looking at her picture and listening to Meatloaf, I felt her spiritual presence. As I felt her spiritual presence, I realized that "My beautiful blonde library angel resides where angels sing!".

This beautiful blonde library angel was my original library angel. She was all that I needed to keep me going back to the library. Sadly, she was not always working at the library and it was during these times that I discovered the four other beautiful angels. Now, I will introduce the other library angels who carried the torch for her when she was not at the library.

The first of these four beautiful library angels were not an obvious choice. This was because she had a very unique look which I found very attractive. This unique looking library angel dressed more like a bookworm than an obvious beauty. I found this look attractive because I felt it showed how comfortable she was with herself. Another reason I was attracted to her was because she always had an air about her of being somewhat introverted and shy. Yet, I also felt that she was very comfortable with her shyness because she was always smiling and greeting people. Also, I saw her laughing and talking with the staff most of the time. One final reason why I was attracted to this angel was that she reminded me of my French soul mate. I even started to think of her as Annabelle 2 because she looked and acted so much like Annabelle.

Annabelle 2 was an important library angel because I thought she might have been interested. I was thinking this because of how she was always smiling at me and saying hello. When a beautiful woman smiles at me and says hello, I will instantly feel this burst of energy. Sadly, this newfound energy quickly turns into fear and anxiety because she might be interested, and I might have to say something to her. I feel this fear and anxiety because she will then learn about my inadequacies. I fear her discovering that I have no religious beliefs and no friends. I fear her finding out about my employment history. Finally, I fear her discovering I have never had a romantic relationship other than my obsessions. I know from my many years of therapy that these negative thoughts are not helpful. I know positive thinking should be my focus. However, this is difficult to do because I feel so undeserving of the attention of beautiful women.

The third of these beautiful library angels was a brunette beauty with freckles. This beautiful brunette library angel was the only one of the library angels to work at the library. All of these other library angels were students who only worked at the library while they were going to college. Thus, she was the only library angel working at the library during the day while the other library angels were going to school. Also, this library angel wore a name tag leading me to be able to refer to her by name. This third library angel was also the most physically attractive. I believe this library angel was of Irish descent because of something my father had mentioned about her having freckles. Obviously, it was not because I asked her. However, the idea of her being Irish or of any European heritage made her that much more attractive. Another reason, I found this library angel so very attractive was that she was so friendly and outgoing. There were a few times when she even said hello to me as I entered the library. However, her greetings stopped when I started to wear my headphones to the library. I could tell how outgoing she was because she was spending hours socializing with the other staff members. I loved this about her, yet I could not understand how she could do this because of my social anxiety. There was yet another reason why this freckled, Irish angel was so special. She was also special because she was the first beautiful angel, I imagined sitting by me at the fireplace of my snowy log cabin. Hence, she was who led me to start imagining the woman of my dreams at my snowy log cabin.

These first three library angels were the three most important of the five beautiful library angels. The fourth library angel was not as obvious a choice because it took a while for another beautiful angel to stand out. There was a black-haired beauty who was not at the library for that much time. The only thing I remember about her was that she was beautiful and friendly. Then there was another attractive brunette who was probably there for a great deal more time. I believe she might have remained at the library for about a year and a few months. This beauty stood out as my fourth library angel for several reasons. One reason why she stood out was because she was very good friends with the beautiful blonde library angel. The reason I believe they were such good friends was because they were always talking to each other at the library. Another reason she stood out was her hair style which reminded me of a cute golden poodle. This was very attractive because it helped enhance her facial features. Finally, it did not hurt that she was very attractive and that she could play a musical instrument. Thus, when I think of this beautiful library angel, I think of her as the creative library angel. Over time, I even started to think that she might have been interested since she started looking my way. The only negative thing about this beauty was that she had tattoos. I could never understand a beautiful woman wanting to ruin her beauty with tattoos. I started to consider her my fourth beautiful library angel, and since she played a musical instrument, I called her my beautiful creative library angel.

Finally, we get to my fifth beautiful library angel. The fifth beautiful library angel was more remembered as the many library angels who worked at the library for a short time and left. There were several attractive library angels who were only briefly at the library or they were too new for me to write about them. I remember one of these beautiful library angels was this brunette with glasses. Finally, there were two new angels, a redhead, and an ebony library angel.

These five beautiful library angels were what kept me returning to the library day after day. It started with the beautiful blonde library angel. She was followed by Annabelle 2. Then, there was the beautiful Irish library angel. My fourth beautiful library angel was the beautiful creative library angel. Finally, the interchangeable library angels were my fifth library angel. Out of these interchangeable library angels, I was to discover the fiery red head. Each one of these library angels were very beautiful women. However, they never were more than obsessions because I was too scared to socialize with them. I saw these beautiful women as only beautiful angels I could admire from a distance. I never once thought about socializing with them because I lacked the confidence to do so. However, I was starting to find some confidence.

I was starting to find some confidence as I started writing about my spiritual journey. I was mostly writing about my beautiful blonde library angel at the start of my journey. However, then I felt her spiritual energy with the other angels when she was not working. Thus, they carried the torch for her so that I could continue to cultivate my writing when she was not there.

My spiritual journey with my beautiful blonde library angel took about two years to develop. This spiritual journey was going to be the story of my first book. However, one thing that I have to stress is that this was only the story of the birth of my passion for writing. This was only the story of its birth since I never saw a day when I did not want to write about it. I believed that writing about my spiritual journey was my reason for living. Thus, I never saw a day when I was not writing about it. I knew I was even going to continue this story once my beautiful blonde library angel left the library forever. Thus, this was why these four other library angels were so pivotal to my spiritual journey. I was starting to find out that each one of these beauties were inspiring my passion for writing in their own special way. They were all increasing the magic of the library by keeping her spiritual energy alive when she was not there.

These five beautiful library angels helped me escape my pit of darkness through my passion for writing. The moment I chose not to shy away from my obsessions with these library angels was the moment my spiritual journey truly started. I could not keep fighting my love for beautiful women anymore. I believed that these obsessions with beautiful women were all I was ever going to have as far as romance unless I started thinking outside the box for a new path. I knew socializing was not working for me, no matter how much I wished I could socialize. Unfortunately, socializing was not going to be one of my strengths because of my social anxiety.

I could not believe that this was my life. I could not believe that I was well into my forties and I had never had a beautiful woman or any type of romantic relationship. I could not believe the closest I got to romance was the blonde from high school who wrote me a letter. Unfortunately, this was my life and I had to accept it. I started my path toward acceptance by changing the way I looked at my obsessions with beautiful women. I was done with feeling embarrassed or ashamed about my love for seeing beautiful women. I wanted to tell the world about my love for them. However, I could not because of my social anxiety. So, I started to write about my love for them and I was not going to stop until I found the woman of my dreams.

This was how my spiritual journey was born. It was born out of an obsession with a beautiful blonde library angel. Then, it continued with me finding four other beautiful angels to obsess over when she was not working. An important change to my inner dialogue was happening as I was following my obsessions with them. I was starting to see these library angels as symbols of hope for what I might attain if I continued my spiritual journey with them. Unfortunately, I knew that I was far from attaining one of these beautiful angels because of my social anxiety. So, I had to accept them as only being my beautiful library angels. Once I accepted this about them, I felt their spiritual energy flow through me as I wrote at the library.

They say the life of a writer is a lonely life. I tend to agree with this statement since the life of a writer is a very lonely life. It has to be a very lonely life because you need to be alone to connect with your true self. To make this connection you must block out all other voices, only then are you able to cultivate your passion for writing and be a great writer. I believe my social anxiety is what allows me to live a lonely life. Do I wish I could have lived a more social life? Of course, I do, however this has not been my life so far. Maybe, it will someday with the confidence I gain from my passion for writing which also helped me escape my pit of darkness.

My Escape From My Pit Of Darkness

My escape from my pit of darkness started with me going to the library to see my beautiful blonde library angel. My discovering her then led to the discovery of my four other beautiful library angels. These five angels inspired me to find my passion for writing. This passion for writing and my obsession with my five beautiful library angels is finally what inspired my escape. The library was the setting for my escape from this mental pit of darkness.

It had been about two months since I fell into my mental pit of darkness. It was also during these two months that I was going to find my new reason for living. My new reason for living was going to be the pursuit of my passion for writing. This pursuit helped me find my way back to the realm of reality. My return to the realm of reality meant that I was going to have to find work again. My need for work had never really disappeared it had only gone dormant while pursuing a future as a truck driver. It did not matter if I had fallen into a mental pit of darkness or whether things were going great, my need for work was always present. This need for work never disappeared because I still needed money to survive. However, as I was finding my escape from this mental pit of darkness, I started reevaluating my life. I started to think about how much money I really needed to survive. I knew I did not have to worry about having money for food or shelter because I was still living with my parents. I had accepted that I was probably never going to move out of my parent's house unless I had a family. I never saw the point of moving out if I did not have a family. I never saw the point because if I was going to pay rent then I wanted to pay it to my parents rather than to some stranger. Sadly, I did not believe I was ever going to have a family because of my social anxiety. I knew that to have a family you had to socialize with beautiful women and to do this I needed confidence. This confidence was something that was lacking from my life before my fall into my pit of darkness.

I believed my life was never going to change when I fell into my pit of darkness. I believed I was always going to live my life alone and without a family. I saw no escaping my pit of darkness, then I discovered my beautiful blonde library angel, and everything changed. I was going to the library whenever I found the time. Then, my obsession with her introduced me to my passion for writing. This introduction to my passion for writing was what turned my obsession with her into something more than a mere obsession with a beautiful woman. After, my obsession with her, my life changed forever because I found my life had purpose. My passion for writing was now my life's purpose and time was my most valuable resource. Time was my most valuable resource because time was how I was able to cultivate my writing. Cultivating my writing was important because it was how I was starting to build my confidence.

My passion for writing was my source of strength. It was helping me to slowly build confidence. Years later, this confidence was going to help me find the courage to approach some beautiful women because my anxiety was so high that I could not sit still anymore. Usually, when I made these approaches I stopped listening to my doubts. So, I approached them without thinking. I still did not believe I could attain these beautiful women. However, I found that every time I approached them my confidence grew more and more. Then, I found myself contradicting the belief I had that I was never going to be able to approach a beautiful woman.

I never wanted to leave my world of isolation. I never wanted to leave my world of isolation because this was where I was starting to build my confidence. Unfortunately, I knew I had to work because I knew I needed to make money. I could not deny my wanting a car anymore. I knew I was still hoping to one day move back to Alaska. I knew I was still hoping to save enough money to buy my snowy log cabin once I moved to Alaska. Finally, I knew I needed to make money to get my book published and to promote my book once it was published.

My escape from my pit of darkness started with me looking into freelance writing. I believed there had to be a way to make money as a writer. Sadly, I was never able to find a way to make money with freelance writing. I was never able to find my way into freelance writing because the information I found about it was too overwhelming and confusing. Also, I felt as if it was only taking time away from me writing the books I hoped to get published someday. Hence, I only saw freelance writing as a distraction from my true passion which was to one day be a published writer. Once I stopped looking into freelance writing, I started spending all my time writing my book. However, this was very time consuming. So, my first obstacle while escaping my pit of darkness was to find out how to pursue my writing while returning to work.

My passion for writing was going well. I had a title and an introduction written for my first book. So now, it was time to shift my focus from my passion for writing to my need for making money. I started to shift my focus by looking into freelance writing. Then after I realized how this was taking too much time away from writing my books, I had to stop. I had to stop to think about how I was going to find the time to do everything. I knew my passion for writing was still the most important thing for my spiritual journey. So, I still needed to find the time to pursue it. I knew I needed to make money, so I had to find the time to work. Then, I started to think about all the other things I wanted to pursue, such as my reading, exercise, reading my positive affirmations, and journaling. I was starting to get overwhelmed by everything I was trying to pursue. This was what led me to a new phase of my spiritual journey.

This new phase of my spiritual journey was going to be about time management. The first part of time management was going to be about me thinking about my priorities. I started to search within myself to figure out what my priorities were as I continued my spiritual journey. This meant I had to block out the rest of the world because what I found important and the rest of the world found important did not match. The rest of the world valued money since they had families to support. However, this was not my life. I had no family to support and I never felt this was going to change because of my social anxiety. Most of the time this was something I found to be very sad and depressing. Then, there were other moments when I felt this was something to celebrate. I found myself celebrating these moments with my passion for writing.

My world of isolation was where I went to manage my time as I started my spiritual journey. The first step toward managing my time was to think about my priorities. I knew my passion for writing was still my top priority and this was never going to change. I knew my passion for music was important because it helped create my world of isolation. My love for Pepsi and the cold were important for this same reason. Finally, I knew how important it was for me to continue my obsession with beautiful women. So, I had to keep returning to the library. Yet, I also knew I had to find work. Thus, I had to see how to find the time to look for work. I was not willing to forego my passion for writing to find work. I was not willing to forego journaling because this helped me to clear my head before I started writing. I did not want to forego reading since I felt it might help me to be a better writer. I believed reading allowed me to gain insight into the minds of other writers. I was not willing to forego anything for work. So, instead of thinking about what to forego, I started planning every minute of every day. I was hoping that this might help me get to everything. However, the problem with making my plans was that making these plans was taking me too much time. I found that trying to make these perfect plans was another distraction from me writing my book. I also felt this was a distraction from me getting work. So, I stopped trying to plan out every minute of every day since it was keeping me from following the path of my spiritual journey. I knew that if I wanted to find employment, I was going to have to leave my world of isolation. Leaving my world of isolation was something difficult for me to do because it meant confronting my social anxiety. I was ready to confront my social anxiety to find work though because I found my passion for writing.

Applying for work was the initial reason I fell into my pit of darkness. I believed that extroverted work was the only work I was ever going to do for the rest of my life. This was not a life I was willing to live because of my social anxiety. These dark thoughts of what my future was going to look like was what led me into my pit of darkness. Then, I was introduced to my passion for writing and I thought I found my path to a better life. I started to create this path with the spiritual energy I felt from my passion for writing. I was introduced to this spiritual energy by my beautiful blonde library angel; however, it was my passion for writing that kept it alive. The spiritual energy I feel from my passion for writing is what keeps my memories of these beautiful angels alive. When I enter my world of isolation, I am able to revisit the spiritual relationships I created with all these beautiful angels. These relationships are all imaginary though because I have never been able to talk to any of them. However, when I enter the imaginary world that I created each and everyone of these spiritual relationships feel quite real.

My world of isolation was a powerful escape at the start of my spiritual journey. I believed this was the only escape I was ever going to have at the start of my spiritual journey. Then, as I spent more time within my world of isolation, I started to find hope. This hope originated from the confidence I was building with my passion for writing. My passion for writing helped me think outside the box to another way of communicating with beautiful women.

This other way required some patience and a powerful belief within my passion for writing. However, I felt I had nothing to lose since I believed that I was never going to have the social skills to get a beautiful woman. I also believed I wanted a beautiful woman more than anything. I accepted these two beliefs as facts at the start of my spiritual journey. Then, I started to think outside the box. I thought about how to attain a beautiful woman if it was not by socializing. I believed that my passion for writing was the only possible way for this to happen.

This belief that my passion for writing might one day lead me to the woman of my dreams was the strength and power of my passion for writing. This was the spiritual energy that was going to power my escape from my pit of darkness. This same spiritual energy was starting to give me the confidence to return to work. I started my return to work by applying to a hundred places. I got about twenty-five applications completed when I was hired as a delivery driver for a sub place. This work was not a great place to work. However, it led me back to the world of work, so I was excited about getting hired to work at this sub place at first. I was studying the menu because I wanted to make a good impression. Sadly, my experience here was not great because I was not getting many hours. Also, I was spending more money for gas than I was getting for tips. Then, there was the fact that I was working with mostly college students which made me uncomfortable. Finally, the assistant manager was making work uncomfortable since he was so stressed. My only relief was when I made deliveries to escape my anxiety. Working at this sub place was not all bad though because there was this beautiful blonde working there who looked like my beautiful blonde library angel. Luckily, I soon found out that they were two different girls. This was a relief since I feared shattering the image, I had of my beautiful blonde library angel by learning that she was not my beautiful perfect angel. This employment that I got at this sub place was going to be my reintroduction to the world of work.

This work at this sub place was my first venture into the world of work as I started my escape from my pit of darkness. My work at this sub place helped me escape my pit of darkness because I started to make some money and deal with humanity again. It also helped me to escape because once I left this work it was not to return to my world of isolation. I left this work for what I was hoping was going to be better work. It was during my second week of work at this sub place that I got an email from a grocery store asking me for a phone interview. I started to get very excited by the idea of working there because I saw it as a place to grow and prosper. Also, I saw this as being a place I could work while pursuing my passion for writing. I felt this was a good place to work because I was going to be getting decent hours yet not too many hours. So, when I learned of their interest, I was ready to put forth all my energy toward getting hired. I responded to the email I got, and I had two days to prepare for my phone interview with them. I chose to stop everything during these two days to learn all I could about this grocery store. Also, I looked over all the possible interview questions. Then, I prepared myself for the interview as much as possible. I spent these two days studying and building my confidence. Then, when it was time for the actual phone interview it went very well. So, they had me go for an interview with the manager of the deli department. I spent another two days studying and building my confidence for this interview. The day of the interview arrived, and I was hired at the interview.

I was looking forward to my new work at this grocery store. I thought working at this grocery store might help me find the right balance between work and my passion for writing. It had been two months since I lost my dream of being a truck driver. However, it had been about a year since I last got a paycheck, so I had been broke for quite some time. I still had a car to pay for which I could not afford. I could not afford the gas or the car insurance for my car, so I was considering letting it sit at home. I thought about cancelling my car insurance until I got work again. I did not want this to happen. However, I was completely broke and there was no possible way I was going to ask my parents for more money. So, I felt this was the best option.

I had one more option before I stopped driving. This option was to work for an employment agency that hired you by the day. Then, when I started to do this work, I realized that it was one of the worst jobs you could possibly imagine. I was doing work in a factory which nobody else wanted for minimum wage and no benefits. I could only tolerate doing this work for about two days. I could not tolerate the heat and the lack of hope for a better future. Also, there was a part of me that was still not ready to go back to work. I still did not want to sacrifice my time for my passion for writing by doing work that made me miserable. I still had my parents and a car, so I was not ready to sacrifice my time for money. Plus, I still had the hope of being able to find better work. Also, I still had my parents to go to for financial support.

My parents were something I was grateful for because they were the reason, I was not desperate for work. I might never have had the best relationships with my parents. However, I was always able to turn to them for financial support. Plus, they always offered me shelter and food. I will always be grateful to them for their financial support. My parents were the reason I was not homeless. They were the reason I have never been desperate to find work. Sadly, though, they were not going to be around forever. So, I needed to find a way to support myself.

My first day of work at this grocery store was the day of orientation. They were hoping that I could start right away which I had no problem with since I needed the money. After I went to orientation, I got my schedule, and I was officially employed at the grocery store. I was hired for the deli department which was the worst department for someone with social anxiety. After orientation, my excitement for working at this grocery store quickly faded away. On my first day of work at the deli department, I could tell I was going to have a difficult time working here. My first day at work the manager had me talking to the customers to take their orders. This made me very uncomfortable and what was worse the manager was not training me at all. As a matter of fact, nobody was training me they simply wanted me to ask questions if I had any. However, I was not someone who wanted to ask questions because I dreaded bringing any type of attention to myself. So, my first day of work at this grocery store my social anxiety was skyrocketing and I had no means of escape. I kept reminding myself of the vision I had for my path as a writer. I kept telling myself this work was a steppingstone toward my future as a writer, however my social anxiety was making my life there miserable. Surprisingly, I found helping customers to be the best part of this work. I felt that this was the best part because helping customers meant I did not have to deal with the manager or any of the other employees.

I was finally fired from this grocery store for being late. This was the reason why management told me I was fired. However, I knew the real underlying reason why I was fired from this grocery store was because of my social anxiety. I was uncomfortable at work because of a series of events that occurred at work because of my social anxiety. This series of events started with me complaining about my boss to the other employees. I was complaining about her because I felt she was very rude and uncaring. I am not someone who liked to complain about people at work, however I complain because I have nothing else to say. I feel uncomfortable talking about myself because of all of my inadequacies. Thus, when I am at work complaining is the only thing, I am able to say to people. I will usually start complaining because of my boredom.

My boss learned about me complaining about her and called me over to ask about it. Then, I started to feel uncomfortable at work because I did not know who to trust anymore. So, this was when I stopped talking to everyone at the grocery store. Unfortunately, I found that remaining silent at the grocery store was not helping either since it made me feel very defensive.

I started to have a bad attitude at work because I thought everyone at the grocery store wanted me gone. I continued to try and keep quiet at work. Yet, the more that I tried not saying anything, the more I started complaining at work because I had nothing else to say. All my complaining gave me a reputation for having a bad attitude at work. This was making it difficult for me to go to work. This discomfort made me late for work most days. I was also uncomfortable at work because I accidentally turned off the refrigerator one night after work. This cost the company a great deal of money since they had to throw away most of the deli products. So yes, I was fired for being late. Yet, I knew it was more due to my social anxiety.

I lasted about two months at this grocery store before getting fired. I started this work with such high hopes and excitement. I was hoping that my work at this grocery store was going to offer me more of an escape from my pit of darkness. I was hoping I might remain at this grocery store until I got my first book published. Sadly, this was not what was going to happen. This loss was not as devastating as was the loss of truck driving though because I now had my passion for writing. My passion for writing helped me deal with all the emotions I was feeling after being fired. I returned to the library after being fired and to my daily routine of doing research, writing, journaling, and applying for any work that I might get after being fired again.

My passion for writing was getting even more powerful after losing this work at the grocery store since it introduced me to its power to heal. It was with its power to heal that I was able to move forward again after losing this work at the grocery store. The one great thing to derive from the loss of my work was that it gave me more time to cultivate my writing. I saw getting fired as another sign that I was following the right path with my spiritual journey. I knew I was going to have to find work again after losing my work at the grocery store. So, I started the process of applying for work again. This time it took me about two months before I found work again. However, I did not fall back into my pit of darkness as I started this search again because I had my beautiful library angels and my passion for writing to keep me motivated. I knew that working was important since I needed money. However, I also knew about the importance of time since it was only with time that I was able to cultivate my passion for writing.

My Passion For Writing

My passion for writing saved me from falling into another pit of darkness. I saw the following two months of unemployment as an opportunity to strengthen my passion for writing. My plans were to strengthen my passion for writing during these two months by developing a better routine for me to get to my passion for writing. I started to create this better routine by following my gut instincts about what my priorities were when I started my spiritual journey. My new routine at the library after losing my work at the grocery store was not going to change much from my old routine at the library before starting my work at this grocery store. The only change to this new routine was going to be with the importance of cleaning. Cleaning was always something I hated having to do since it felt like work without the benefit of getting paid. Thus, cleaning was never one of my top priorities. Yet, it was one of my mother's top priorities. Therefore, I always felt it was something I had to find time to get to for my mother's sake. At least, this was how I felt before being introduced to my passion for writing. Then, once introduced to my passion for writing this all changed since cleaning was not a priority anymore.

The routine that I was going to follow once introduced to my passion for writing was going to reflect my priorities more. This meant a change to my old daily routine because after I left the grocery store my priorities were changing. My priorities were starting to reflect what I felt was important more than what others found important. I started to realize that cleaning was much less of a priority to me because I needed more time for my passion for writing. I had no problem with going home to a messy house since I rarely went home anyways. I was spending most of my time at my locations of inspiration. So, the only cleaning I cared about was doing the laundry, the dishes, taking out the garbage, and taking care of the pets. Then, if I could manage to find extra time, I tried to do some of the other cleaning that my mom found important.

I never wanted to leave my world of isolation. I never wanted to stop cultivating my passion for writing. I wanted to spend every minute of every hour within my world of isolation cultivating my passion for writing. I never felt more alive than when I was cultivating my passion for writing within my world of isolation. Sadly, I could not spend all of my time there because of the guilt I was feeling when I left this world. I was feeling this guilt because I was not cleaning the house to help my mom more. I was feeling guilty because I was not working and making more money to help my mother with the finances more. I was feeling guilty since I was not socializing with beautiful women more while writing at my locations of inspiration. Finally, I was feeling guilty because I felt I was wasting my life because I did not have a family.

This guilt was something that ate away at me whenever I left my world of isolation. I had to find a way to deal with this guilt that I was feeling. I turned to my passion for writing as a way to deal with the guilt. My passion for writing was a great way to deal with the guilt that I was feeling because once I entered my world of isolation my feelings of guilt disappeared. Honestly, once I entered my world of isolation all negative feelings I was having disappeared.

All I felt when I entered my world of isolation was joy and inspiration. This joy and inspiration was all I was feeling because of the five elements that created my world of isolation. My beautiful angels were the eye candy for my world of isolation. My passion for music was what gave this world life. My passion for writing was my way of expressing myself within this world. My Pepsi was reenergizing my world every time I took a sip of its sweetness. Lastly, the cold took me to another spiritual plane while within this world. I never got enough of my time within this world. This world of isolation was where I was finding the strength and confidence to pursue my passion for writing. The more time that I was spending within my world of isolation, the more I started to believe that there had to be a way to make money from this world.

I was the only person who was going to make my dream of being a writer a reality. I believed that the only way that I was going to make it as a writer was if I was selfish. I had to be selfish because I had to ignore what the rest of the world found important to make it as a writer. By the rest of the world, I mostly meant my mother and employers. So, I started to prioritize my plans to reflect what I felt was important rather than what the rest of the world found important. This was a difficult thing for me to do at first though since I felt guilty about not helping others out more. This was a guilt I was going to have to learn to live with if I ever hoped to get to what I found important. There simply was not enough time to do everything. So, I knew I had to reevaluate my priorities if I was going to have any hope of ever making it as a successful writer.

I believed I was going to have to live a selfish life to make it as a writer. I believed I needed to live a selfish life because what I found important was not what others found important. According to my mother, cleaning the house and making money was important. According to my father, making money was important. According to my employers, making money and following the rules were important. According to the rest of the world, having a family as well as making money were important. I did not necessarily disagree with the rest of the world about what was important. I simply disagreed that these were the most important things. I found my time was the most important thing since it was how I was able to cultivate my writing. So, after losing my work at the grocery, I spent all my time at the library. During this time at the library, I was thinking about how I was going to find the time for my priorities. I started to think about how good my writing got when I spent more time cultivating it. This made it difficult for me to return to work and to keep work after I returned. However, I knew that I had to return to work to make money. I knew my need or want for money was never going to disappear. Also, I knew my passion for writing was not going anywhere. Thus, I spent more time cultivating my writing at the library with the belief that someday writing might lead to making money. It was also during these months at the library that I thought about the influence my parents had upon my life.

I will never be able to fully escape the influence my parents had upon my life. My parents shaped me into the person I am today. I first thought about the influence that my father had upon my life during these two months of being out of work. I thought about how he was living his life influenced how I was living life. My father spent the second half of his life doing the things which brought him the most enjoyment. He spent his days sitting downstairs within the garage watching television and drinking. This was all he cared about doing for the rest of his life. He did not care about getting work. He did not care about cleaning. He did do some of the cooking and gardening since they were activities he enjoyed doing when he was able to do them. My father spent the last part of his life doing things he loved not caring about the rest of the world. I spent most of my life resenting my father for living this kind of life. I remember getting into many arguments with him because I felt he could do so much more with his life. However, this was the way he chose to live his life. As I thought about how I wanted to live life and how he lived the last years of his life, I felt there were many similarities. After realizing these similarities, I lost my resentment for him and started to feel jealous about how he lived his life.

I never found joy within the same things that he enjoyed. I never loved the taste of alcohol and I never found any joy from getting drunk. I never liked cooking because I hated the heat, although I did like the sense of pride that I got from cooking a good meal if I had the time. I never liked gardening for the same reason as I never liked cooking, the heat. Finally, I did not like to sit around and watch TV all day anymore since I had my passion for writing. However, this was one of my favorite ways to pass my time before I was introduced to it. Thus, my father's influence was not about the activities he loved. It was more about how he lived his life.

I learned the value of making sacrifices from my mother. I always felt sympathetic toward my mother because she had the daunting task of being the responsible parent. My mother being the responsible parent was why my father could spend his time doing what he enjoyed. So, my mother was as much a role model as was my father. My father introduced me to the importance of following your passions. Whereas my mother introduced me to the importance of being responsible so that you were able to pursue your passion or passions. The older I got, the more I learned of the world. The more that I learned of the world, the more I saw that my mother never had a fair life because of the sacrifices she had to make for both me and my father.

My mother was my role model for being responsible. I always had a more resentful relationship with my mother because she was always stressing responsibility. She was always telling me not to do this and not to do that which made me more resentful of her. This resentment I had toward her was not fair. However, this was how I felt, and I could not blink away my feelings. Before I found my passion for writing, my way of dealing with my feelings toward my mother was through repressed anger. My anger toward my mother was mostly repressed because we never expressed our feelings. I believe we never expressed our feelings because we both have social anxiety. At least, I know I have social anxiety. I am not very certain about my mother having social anxiety because we never discussed this with each other.

The only way our repressed anger was expressed was when it finally erupted like a volcano. This led to many heated arguments and then to us not talking for days. Before finding my passion for writing, I did not have an outlet for my repressed anger. Thus, the repressed anger that I was feeling toward her was turning into resentment. Then, when I was introduced to my passion for writing, I had an outlet to express my anger toward her. As I wrote about my repressed anger toward her, I was able to see that my resentment toward her was not really fair. I saw that she was simply doing what needed to be done by being the responsible parent. I realized it was because she was responsible that my father was able to live the life he had chosen. So, my passion for writing helped me to realize that both my parents taught me valuable lessons before I started my spiritual journey. My mother taught me the importance of responsibility. Whereas my father taught me all about the importance of living life for your passion or passions.

My spiritual journey started with me learning these two valuable lessons from my parents. It continued with me trying to find a way to balance the time I needed to spend at work with the time I wanted to pursue my passion for writing. The loss of my work at the grocery store was an important step toward me finding a way to balance both responsibility and passion. Losing my work at this grocery store allowed me to have more time to cultivate my passion for writing. I spent most of this time writing about the influence my parents had over my life before discovering my passion for writing. Then, I spent the rest of my time writing about beautiful women. The library hours were ten to eight and I was spending every hour at the library writing.

The first book I ever wrote was not very good. Every chapter was about something different. Also, it was very choppy and had no direction or flow. However, completing my first book was an important step toward me being a successful writer. The reason why it was an important step was because it taught me that to find success as a writer, you had to keep writing.

I knew the only way I was going to be a successful writer was if I kept writing. I had many doubts and concerns about finding success as a writer when I started this spiritual journey. However, the one thing I never doubted was my passion for writing. So, I kept writing despite my doubts and concerns because I believed I was going to find success if I simply kept writing. What I did not know though was what this success was going to look like when it finally did arrive. I did not realize that my first glimpse into finding success as a writer simply meant that I was going to start to feel more confident. I believe this confidence is my first sign of success because I am approaching beautiful women and I will be starting work where I have to socialize.

I believed that my path toward being a great writer was very simple at the start of my spiritual journey. I believed that my path toward being a successful writer was to simply write and never stop writing. I believed that writing was the only way to grow as a writer. Thus, I wrote my way through my doubts and fears about getting my first book published. I wrote my way through my fear of never getting the woman of my dreams. I wrote my way through my anxiety about having to return to work. I wrote my way through my fear of never being able to make money as writer. It is now four years later, and I am still writing my way through my fear and anxiety because my fear and anxiety will never go away. However, neither will my passion for writing. I believe that if I continue to write, a solution to my doubts and fears will always present itself. So, my goal at the start of my spiritual journey was to simply get my book completed. I did not care about the quality of the book, I only cared about completing my book.

I believed that completing my very first book was going to be a great boost to my confidence. I was so right! Completing my very first book was a great boost to my confidence. However, as great as it felt to complete my first book, I knew I was nowhere near ready to publish my first book. I knew I was nowhere near ready to publish my first book because this first book I wrote was not very good. My first book was simply a twenty-chapter book about different topics. I am not sure how many pages my first book was because some chapters were only five to ten pages, while others were twenty pages. So, after completing my first book I decided to start over and write a new book. I learned a great deal about the writing process as I wrote my first book. I learned that the content of the material I was writing was very good. I also learned that my writing only got better, the more time I spent writing. For example, I found out that if I started writing around noon then I started to do my best writing around two. Therefore, the most important thing I learned after writing my first book was the value of time.

Time and isolation were my most valuable resources during the writing process. Time was my most valuable resource because it was my way of cultivating my writing. Yet, isolation was also important because the less I was distracted the more thoughts I was able to uncover. So, my social anxiety was my initial reason for not speaking to the beautiful angels that I found myself obsessing over. However, as I continued my spiritual journey with them, I found that a part of the strength of their spiritual energy originated from me not speaking to them. I saw these library angels as symbols for what I hoped to one day attain if I could build my confidence.

I was building this confidence through my passion for writing. My hope was that my obsessions with these beautiful angels might one day lead to a relationship with any one of them. I knew this day was still far away though since I was rarely able to approach a beautiful woman. So, I had to rely upon my passion for writing to give my life purpose. At the start of my spiritual journey, I found that my passion for writing was helping me to realize two dreams. The first dream that it was helping me to realize was my dream of attaining the woman of my dreams. The second dream that it was helping me to realize was my dream of being a successful writer.

I always knew the title of my first book was going to be *The Beautiful Blonde Library Angel.* This was something that never changed as I was writing my first book. I was confident that I had produced some good material for my first book as well. My first book included an introduction and the start of nineteen chapters. Each of these nineteen chapters represented nineteen different topics. There was a chapter about what I was grateful for and a chapter about my wonderful French childhood. Also, I had written a chapter about my discovery of the beautiful blonde library angel and my love for watching television. After writing these chapters, I found that I was feeling quite confident that these chapters had some well written material. Unfortunately, I could not say the same thing about the direction and the flow of my first book.

I had many doubts about the direction and flow of my first book. I had these doubts about the direction and flow of my first book because I isolated each chapter for a different topic. I discovered that isolating each chapter was not helping the flow of my writing. I found that every time I had a thought, I was trying to find the right chapter to write down this thought. Then, as I searched for the right chapter, I lost what it was I wanted to write down. This taught me that it was important to live within the moment when you were writing. I found it was important to live within the moment because being a good writer was about direction and flow.

Separating each chapter of my book into different topics was not working since it was interrupting the flow of my writing. I knew I had to find a way to get my writing to flow better if I wanted to grow as a writer. So, after completing my first book, I knew my first book was not going to reach an audience. Even so, I had no intention of quitting the writing process. It was the start of 2017 and I started to write another version of my first book. I saw my first book as nothing more than a learning process for how to move forward. One of the most important things I learned was how important it was to continue to write. I wrote many more books before I finally realized the story of the first book I was going to publish. I must have written three versions of my book about my life before I started writing the book I was going to try to publish.

It was during my time of unemployment after getting fired from the grocery store that I wrote the first version of my book. This time of being out of work was great for my passion for writing. However, I knew that all this time I had to cultivate my writing could not continue. I knew that it was only a matter of time before I had to return to work. I dreaded the idea of returning to the world of work though because I knew this meant confronting my social anxiety.

I knew I had to return to the world of work. I had to return to the world of work to publish my first book. I never did consider going the route of traditional publication because of my fear of rejection. Thus, self-publication was the only route I saw as a viable option for publishing my first book. So, I started to research self-publication while I was out of work. However, I did not spend too much time researching it since I knew I first had to have a book to publish. So, my new routine at the library consisted of me looking for some type of work and writing my books. Plus, I still wanted to keep reading and journaling during my time at the library. Sadly, finding the time to do all these things at the library was difficult while working.

I also applied for Social Security during these two months out of work because it was something both my therapist and BVR recommended. I never did think I was going to qualify for Social Security benefits though since I knew all the hoops you had to go through to get it. Yet, I still believed that it was something worth pursuing since I had nothing to lose by applying. After all, I definitely felt like I qualified since I had social anxiety, depression, migraines, and OCD. I felt as if any one of these disabilities could qualify me for getting some type of benefits.

I started the process of applying for Social Security by going to the Social Security website and filling out the application. I filled out the application and I completed the paperwork that they needed. This was followed by the calls from people who reviewed all of the cases to see if I was able to get the Social Security benefits. I answered their questions about having social anxiety and migraines and the waiting process started. Finally, I found out I was rejected.

Their rejection letter meant that I was going to have to think about how to return to the world of work once more. The idea of getting regular employment was what led me to my first pit of darkness. My beautiful blonde library angel guided me out of this pit of darkness by giving birth to my spiritual journey whose path was going to be paved by my passion for writing.

My Near Fall Into A Second Pit Of Darkness

My time of being out of work after losing my work at the grocery store led to my near fall into a second pit of darkness. It was during the two months of September and October that I found myself out of work. I spent most of this time cultivating my passion for writing. So, this time of being out of work was great for my passion for writing. However, the more time that I was spending out of work, the closer I was getting to falling into another pit of darkness. I got close to falling into a second pit of darkness when I could not find work after two months. I applied to about a hundred places and I only got twenty interviews. Sadly, none of these interviews turned into work though and I was starting to fear that I might never find work again.

This was the first time that I had ever applied to a hundred places without having any luck of finding work. I was starting to worry that this work at the grocery store might be the last place I might ever work again. I knew all about my poor work history. I knew all about my history of calling off from work so much because of my social anxiety. At times, I did not even call to let my employers know that I was not going to work because of it. I was starting to fear that all these employers knew about my poor work history. Thus, my fear was that none of these employers were going to take a risk at hiring me ever again. This was what almost led me to my second pit of darkness. The only reason why I did not fall into another pit of darkness was because of my passion for writing. Yet, after my first month of not finding work I was getting desperate for work and this desperation nearly led me into my second pit of darkness. Again, this was the first time I applied to a hundred places without finding work. Usually, I got to about fifty applications and found some type of work. Sadly, this was not the case this time. My time of unemployment was causing me a great deal of fear and anxiety about not finding any work. This fear and anxiety I was feeling was what led me to my near fall into a second pit of darkness.

My passion for writing kept me from falling into a second pit of darkness. I did not believe that I was ever going to fall into another pit of darkness if I had my passion for writing. The loss of my hearing, my vision, my fingers, or death were the only way that I saw myself falling into another pit of darkness. Otherwise, I knew I could find some way to move forward.

My time of being unemployed was helping me to enrich my passion for writing. I completed most of my first book during this time of being out of work. Unfortunately, as great as this time off was for my passion for writing, I knew I had other areas of my life to improve. Thus, I started to take the confidence I was gaining from my passion for writing and I started to apply it to improving the other areas of my life. One area of my life I wanted to improve was educating myself through self-help books again. So, I started to devote some of my time of being out of work to reading self-help books while at the library. Some of the self-help books I read were about ways to improve one's confidence and how to change your way of thinking. I also started to read romance novels since I was starting to think about writing a romance novel. Finally, I was also reading books about how to get my book published. I spent about an hour a day reading these books to improve my life. I felt it was important for me to keep reading because I felt it was giving me insight into how other writers were cultivating their writing skills.

I was never bored during my time of being unemployed because there was always something for me to write and a book for me to read. However, reading and writing were not the only things occupying my time. I was also still spending most of my time journaling and trying to find work. I was still spending my time journaling because it was helping me clear my mind before I started cultivating my passion for writing. Then, I was spending the rest of this time looking for employment because I knew that I still needed money. I knew that as much as I valued my time to cultivate my passion for writing, money was also still something that I needed.

I was feeling the importance of money when I saw how restricted my life was getting because I was lacking the financial means to do certain things. I knew I needed money to keep a car because I needed to pay for gas and for the car insurance every month. I also had to save money to get my book published once I wrote it. Thus, my struggle between finding the time to cultivate my passion for writing and my need for work continued. I knew that as this battle continued, I was going to need to find a way to find balance to both sides of the battle. However, finding this balance was not going to happen right away. I found that finding the time for my passion for writing was not much of a struggle since this was my favorite way of passing time. However, I found that it was much more of a struggle for me to find the time to get and keep work because this was something I had to do rather than something I wanted to do with my life.

My struggle to find work again continued after having applied to a hundred places with no luck. I continued my fight to find work again by going over my list of a hundred applications and I started to apply to more places to replace some of the more dreadful places that I applied. Then, as I returned home from the library one night my father told me about a work fair they were having. I went to this work fair preparing myself for disappointment because my past experiences with work fairs were very disappointing. However, I felt I had to go to this work fair because I had exhausted all other avenues of finding work. So, I went to the work fair dressed professionally with a pair of black slacks, a tie, dress shoes, and a pressed white shirt. I printed out twenty of my resumes to give out to employers at the work fair. Then, when I got their I knew I was as prepared as could be, yet my anxiety was still through the roof. It was through the roof since I knew I was going to have to talk to potential employers when I got there. Also, I felt I was too underqualified to apply to any of these places. I decided to ignore my anxiety though since I knew I needed work. So, I started walking around the work fair once I got there and talking to some potential employers. I was trying the best I could to appear both presentable and confident while talking to them. I was walking around and stopping at any place I had the slightest interest of working. I was looking to return to the refrigerated factory I was working at since this was where I first found out about them. Sadly, they were not there. So, I was about ready to leave since I felt so underqualified to work at any of these places. Then, right before I left, I was feeling some hope and confidence return. I was feeling this hope and confidence return with my passion for writing as I was reminded of how it gave my life purpose.

My passion for writing gave me the hope and confidence I needed to return to work. It gave me this hope and confidence by reminding me of why it was that I was returning to work. I knew finding work again was only a way for me to achieve success as a writer. So, I knew my main reason for returning to work was to pay for my book to be published. Thus, I returned to the work fair and made one last attempt at finding work. As I walked around this time, I was feeling much more at ease while talking to employers since I lost my desperation for work. The need for work was still present because I still needed to make money. However, my need to make money was not my priority anymore. I knew finding time for my writing was my priority.

I had a few interviews that I thought went very well once I returned to the work fair. I left the work fair feeling more hopeful and confident about my chances of finding work. I went to the library after the work fair and I started journaling about my experience at the work fair. Then, when I got home, I learned I got three calls from places that wanted to a phone interview.

One of these places was from a call center. This call center sent me an email for a day and time to have a phone interview. The phone interview went well, and I had an appointment the following week for another interview with one of the supervisors. The second place who called was this drug and alcohol rehab center. This phone interview also went well. Thus, I now had two interviews to speak to supervisors. Finally, I had one final phone interview with a company who took care of people with physical disabilities. This final phone interview was to also go well. As a matter of fact, this last interview went so well that this was going to be the work that I was going to eventually accept. So, it was a good thing I decided to return to the work fair since it led to me having three interviews and eventually to my new work. Unfortunately, my return to work also meant the return of the anxiety I felt about having to work.

I had this anxiety about having to return to work because I was going to have to talk to people at work. My social anxiety at work is another reason why I feel my passion for writing is so important. I believe my success as a writer will lead me to another way of making money besides having to go to work and socialize with people every day. My life as a writer will not lead me to being free of ever having to confront my social anxiety. I know there will be times when I will have to confront it to make money as a writer. I believe that part of being a successful writer will involve book readings and answering questions. However, I know from past experiences that I am able to give presentations and talk to groups of people. Sure, these social situations are uncomfortable. However, I am able to control this social anxiety because I have time to prepare for these social situations. The times I feel I have trouble confronting my social anxiety are when I have to be vulnerable and talk about my personal life. Therefore, the times when I feel the most uncomfortable are during unstructured situations because I fear they will lead to people asking me personal questions about my life. I found that there are some things I feel comfortable talking about though, such as my passions. I am able to talk about my love for France, my passion for music, watching TV, and my passion for writing. The moments when I feel uncomfortable arise when we have to change topics. I find when I have to change topics, my mind will go blank since I do not know how to start a new topic. This leads to those moments of awkward silences. It will be all these moments of awkward silences and my debilitating social anxiety that continue to lead me to try and find ways to avoid social situations.

I have lived my entire life avoiding social situations because of this social anxiety. My debilitating social anxiety was something that I thought I was never going to be able to escape. I knew that the only way to get over my social anxiety was to confront it. Sadly, placing myself within unstructured situations where I must be vulnerable was also my greatest fear. I feared unstructured situations even more than I feared dying alone. Thus, my social anxiety was a disability that I feared I was going to have to live with for the rest of my life. I never thought I was going to find relief from my social anxiety because it was my life's handicap. I have two handicaps that plague my life. My migraines and my social anxiety are two of my life's handicaps. I believe the only way to live with my two life handicaps is to somehow accept them.

I knew from my past experiences I was never going to have any great success at work because of my social anxiety. I knew that regular work meant extroverted work. This meant me having to socialize with coworkers and customers which was my greatest fear. I also knew I needed money though, so I had to keep at it. I had to keep working. However, I knew where this path was going to lead every time. Thus, I went into these employment situations knowing what to expect. I knew that I was never going to be able to keep extroverted work for a great deal of time because of my social anxiety. Thus, I started to think outside the box if I wanted success. Thinking outside the box meant me not being disappointed if I was unable to remain at work because of my Social Anxiety. More importantly, thinking outside the box meant my focusing more attention and time toward my passion for writing since it was my way to success.

I believed if I was ever going to find any type of success then it was only going to be through my passion for writing. My passion for writing was helping me to accept the fact that I was never going be a very sociable person. It helped me accept that the best I could ever do socially was to merely find a way to survive. For me, I saw a successful day as merely being a day when I was able to leave my house for any reason. Thus, for me I was gaining confidence by simply going to my locations of inspiration to see my beautiful angels. I knew that the chances of me talking to them was unlikely, however I had no chance of talking to them at home.

My inability to express myself verbally was what led me to finding my passion for writing. My passion for writing was the most important thing to my life after I was introduced to its power by my beautiful blonde library angel. My passion for writing was so important because it was my only way of telling people about my social anxiety. Thus, my passion for writing was going to give my life meaning and purpose by helping me to express myself. My passion for writing was also helping me find the confidence to return to work. I was finally starting to get the opportunity to return to the world of work after I risked going to this work fair.

I knew I had to return to work if I wanted to continue to pursue my dream of being a published writer because I was going to have to pay to get my first book published. I knew my main reason for wanting to find success as a writer was that I hated socializing at work. So, I was starting to see my return to work as a way to live a better future. A future where I did not have to confront my social anxiety as much anymore unless I wanted to confront it. Thus, I knew my ultimate goal during my spiritual journey was to get some books published. Then, the second step was to start making money with these published books. The first step to make this happen though was to return to the world of work to make money. I knew that once I found success as a writer, I was going to have the financial means to spend more time writing. So, I was looking for a way to return to the world of work at the work fair. I was looking for employment because I saw this as the start of my path toward a better future. The one thing that I knew was never going to change during my spiritual journey was my passion for writing. Unfortunately, work was also important, and I was at a point when I had to do extroverted work.

This work fair that I went to was going to help me find three paths for returning to the world of work. This was a great feeling after nearly falling into another pit of darkness. One of my paths back to work was at a call center and another was for this rehab center. However, I eventually chose to work with people with disabilities at their homes. I eventually chose this work since I was guaranteed work there after I had made a great impression during my interview.

The one thing that has always surprised me about looking for work was that I never had trouble with interviews. I guess it was from all the practice that I had over the years since I knew that I was always going to need to make money. So, despite my social anxiety, I never had trouble going to interviews since I was able to fake a good impression. The problem was keeping that fake impression going once I was finally hired and also with following all the rules.

My first interview was with the call center. I got to the interview and did not have the paperwork that they needed. So, I lost the opportunity to interview with them. They told me to reschedule, however I did not bother because the other two interviews went so well. Then, when I went for my interview at the rehab center. This interview went very well, and I probably was going to get hired. However, I was going to have to wait a month to see if my background check went through. I was not willing to wait a month to start making money though since I had not worked for two months and I had no money saved. Thus, my choice was not a difficult choice after these three interviews, I went where I was guaranteed work. Finally, I felt my days of looking for work were over when I started to work with disabled individuals at their homes. I was finally going to make some decent money so that I could start my path toward being a successful writer. I also thought I found work that I might be able to remain at for several years.

My journey back to the world of work continued as I worked with disabled individuals. This return to the world of work meant that I had to find a way to balance my passion for writing with work once again. My two months of being out of work allowed me the time to cultivate my passion for writing. This time spent cultivating my passion for writing was then helping me build my confidence. I needed to have this confidence while working with disabled individuals.

My interview to work with disabled people went surprisingly well. I always did well at interviews. However, this interview went really well, and the shocking thing was that this time it had nothing to do with preparation since I was not even going to go to the interview. Before I had the interview, I felt so underqualified that I had no plans of even going to the interview. As I was driving to the interview, I made a detour to go to my Depression Support Group instead. I had my interview appointment set for a Tuesday which was the same day as my support groups. Thus, I found myself spending part of my drive to the interview going back and forth between my support group and the interview. Then, I had the same feeling I got before leaving the work fair. I felt this sense of hope and confidence flow through me and I decided to go for the interview because I had nothing to lose. Finally, after my mind-consuming drive there, I arrived.

I finally arrived and let them know that I was ready for the interview. I waited for the interviewers. As I was waiting there, I started to feel a sense of calmness flow through me like at the work fair. This was a feeling of who cares what happens because I knew it was only a steppingstone toward my passion for writing. It was a feeling of I had no chance anyways, so I might as well gain some practice from the interview. Finally, the interviewers arrived to take me to the interview and as I was walking to the interview, I felt my anxiety disappear. Then, as the interview started, I felt a sense of confidence rather than my normal anxiety. I did not feel the pressure of having to do well during the interview since I did not think I had a shot. This feeling of confidence was a feeling I had not felt since the work fair and I went with it. I started the interview with this feeling of confidence, and it was going to remain during the entire interview.

The interview went great. I started walking toward the office where the interview was going to take place. The room where we had the interview had a round table for us to sit at. As I entered the room, I found out that there were going to be two interviewers rather than one. However, this did not phase me because I was still feeling this sense of calmness and confidence. I was also not phased by the fact that the interviewers were two people that normally made me very uncomfortable. I was being interviewed by someone reminding me of a school bully and a beautiful woman. Thus, under normal circumstances I might have been intimidated by them, however not this time. The confidence I was feeling allowed me to block out all the anxiety and fear I normally might be feeling. So, I was able to answer the questions with a clear mind. The interviewers must have been impressed because they had me take the essay portion of the interview. Then, they had me go back to the waiting room while they looked over my essay. Finally, I was told that they wanted me to go for a second interview with the director of one of the group homes. I was starting to feel my sense of calmness and confidence disappear before the second interview started. I was starting to feel the need to escape because I remembered all the things, I was telling myself before the interview. Then, the second interview started, and I was able to do well enough during the second interview to get hired. The entire interview process took about four hours. Before I had the interview, I felt I had no chance of being hired, then after the interview I felt I had a good chance of being hired. I felt I had a good chance because they already gave me a schedule. I was only waiting for a background check before I could work with disabled individuals at a group home. Finally, once I got home, I soon discovered that I was hired which meant that I was finally ready to return to the world of work.

The World Of Work

My journey back to the world of work continued with me finding employment with a group home. This employment with a group home was causing me a great deal of anxiety. I was feeling this anxiety because I had to care for individuals with disabilities at this group home. I started feeling this anxiety the moment orientation started because of all we had to learn. Our two weeks of orientation consisted of a self-defense class and a CPR class. Then, we had van training and we had to learn to pass out medication to our clients as well. There were so many rules and procedures that we had to learn before I was ready to work at my first group home. Thus, most of my time during class was spent absorbing all of this information. During orientation, I also found that there was a great deal of time for us to talk about our personal lives.

I was always very uncomfortable when there was time for us to talk about anything personal because of all my inadequacies. It was during this time of socializing that everyone started talking about their family life and their experiences as caretakers. These were things I could not relate to since I did not have a family and I had no experience as a caretaker. So, although, I was bored by all the lectures during class, I always preferred it to having to socialize.

I did the best I could to complete this orientation despite my boredom and my social discomfort. I did the best I could because I thought that if I started to work at this group home, I was going to be able to learn how to be more responsible. So, I was taking as many detailed notes as I could during training to try to decrease my anxiety. I was feeling this anxiety because I had never taking care of another person before other than myself. So, I was hoping these notes might help decrease my anxiety. Then, after class, I went to the library to look over some of the handouts from class and to take some notes. Also, I was researching ways to ease my fear and anxiety about having to be a caretaker. I found that all of this research and studying was helping me keep my fears and anxiety at bay. Sadly, this fear and anxiety was going to return after training, yet I refused to quit my work at group homes since I thought it was helping me to grow.

I was hoping that my work at a group home was going to help me to grow as an individual by helping me to learn more about responsibility. I always felt a great deal of fear and anxiety when I thought about being responsible. I felt this fear and anxiety because I felt being more responsible meant dealing with more and more people. Hence, I never wanted to learn more responsibility because of my social anxiety. Yet, I was also aware of how the rest of the world viewed responsibility. I knew the rest of the world thought that someone was a better person if they held more responsibility. I never understood this view though when I saw how stressed these people got the more their responsibility increased. This stress then led to people rushing, being impatient, getting angry, and ultimately being more miserable. I, for one, was not willing to live my life this way when I knew that my life's handicaps caused me so much misery. So, my view of responsibility and the rest of the world's view of responsibility never matched. My view of responsibility was that it gave you more to do and made you miserable. The rest of the world viewed it as being something that made you a better person. Sadly, I knew I had to temporarily adopt the rest of the world's view of being responsible. At least, until I was a writer.

I saw my work at a group home as a way for me to learn responsibility. I thought it was important for me to learn how to be more responsible if I ever wanted a family. Yet, honestly, I never really cared that much about having a family. One reason why I never cared much about having a family was because I feared this meant letting go of your dreams. Thus, as I thought about my reasons for being depressed, I knew that having a family was not one of them. My reasons for being depressed were more about not having a girlfriend. Yet, I also knew how beautiful women valued responsibility because most beautiful women wanted to have a family.

I was looking forward to my work at a group home because I was hoping to learn about responsibility. I knew being a caretaker was going to require me to be more responsible because I was going to be taking care of individuals with disabilities. Yet, being more responsible was also causing me a great deal of anxiety. I was feeling this anxiety because I feared where this path of learning responsibility might lead. I feared that it might take me away from my passion for writing and my dream of someday being a writer. Upon looking back at this path, I do not think this was the right path for me to take. I knew I was going to learn about responsibility working at group homes, however I also knew that this work was keeping me from my writing.

I knew that any path that took me away from my writing was the wrong path. My passion for writing was what gave my life its meaning and purpose. So, if working at a group home and learning to be more responsible was taking me away from this path, it was not the right path. However, I was not aware of this at the time. So, as I started my training with orientation, I was going to put forth my best effort because I felt it was the right path at the time.

My two weeks of training during orientation was the start of my new path towards success at a group home. I saw this work as being my path toward learning responsibility and then one day attaining a beautiful woman. This path was not going to be a successful path though because I was going to have so much car trouble. My car troubles started during my two weeks of training. It was a cold and snowy day during the month of December when my car troubles started. It was during one of these cold and snowy days that I went to start my car with no luck. I could hear the engine start. Unfortunately, I could not get it to kick into gear. I spent about a half an hour turning the key trying to get the engine to start with no luck. Finally, I had to stop trying and call work to let them know my car was not starting. So, I had no way of getting to class, and at first, they told me that class was mandatory. Thus, I had to find a way to get to class. I went to my car to see if I could somehow get it to start with no luck again. Finally, I called work to let them know I could not make it and I had to reschedule my training.

My car troubles were going to continue for about two months after this cold day of December. These car troubles were going to eventually lead to the loss of my car and the loss of my work at a group home, however I was not aware of this at the time. All I knew at the time was that my car was not starting, and I had to take it to my mechanic to get it repaired. So, I had it towed and my mechanic got it started. Then, I continued with training and I kept trying to get my car repaired as it continued to break down over and over again. Finally, I completed my two weeks of training and I started to work at the group home. I was feeling a great deal of anxiety about working there though since I knew I was going to have to be more responsible. Then, there were the repeated car troubles that I was having which were not helping with my anxiety. However, I refused to let this anxiety that I was feeling about learning responsibility or my repeated car troubles stop me from working at this group home. So, I continued to move forward with my work there. I kept hoping that eventually my car was going to get repaired. Then, I was hoping to pay back my mother for the repairs while also saving to publish my book. Unfortunately, I was going to soon learn that this was never going to happen when I lost my car.

My first week of work at this group home was during Christmas. I was scheduled to work at nine and I did not get off until ten. They had me scheduled to work the entire weekend of Christmas and I was dreading this schedule because Christmas was my favorite holiday. However, I knew how much I needed the money, so I knew I was going to have to find a way to learn how to deal with having to work through Christmas. So, I started to think about ways I might still enjoy Christmas while being trapped at work. The first thing I did was I thought about what it was that I was really going to miss about Christmas. I knew that my favorite thing about Christmas was the music, so I brought a radio to work to listen to Christmas music. Another thing I knew I loved about Christmas was watching Hallmark Christmas movies all weekend, so

I had them playing within the background. I was trying to keep the magic of Christmas alive while being trapped at work. However, it was still not a very merry Christmas.

My work schedule was not a horrible schedule once I got through Christmas. I was looking forward to the idea of getting every other weekend off and working shorter work weeks. Also, the work I had to do at the group homes was not all that bad. Sure, there were things I hated doing there, such as cleaning the disabled individuals after they went to the bathroom. I did not know how I was going to be able to tolerate this when I also had OCD. However, what made it tolerable was knowing that I was going to have so much down time while there. This down time made my time at the group home worthwhile since I had time to cultivate my writing.

I thought I had found another good place to work while pursuing my passion for writing. Unfortunately, my work at a group home was not going to last because my car troubles returned.

My car troubles returned during my second weekend of working at this Group home. My car troubles did not start again until after I got to work. They did not start again until it was time for me to get a Polar Pop after I had been at work for about two hours. I was scheduled to work for four hours that Friday night. So, I got to work at about four and then went for my Pepsi about two hours later. Unfortunately, I was not going to get my Pepsi because my car was not going to start again. Instead, I was going to be stuck at the group home the entire weekend without an escape since my car did not start, and it was only my second weekend of work there. So, I knew that it was unfair to ask my mother to go back and forth every day when she also had to go to work. I could not afford a cab because I was so broke after all of the car repairs. Therefore, I was trapped at this group home all weekend because I also could not lose this work.

I was still hoping to repair my car after my second weekend of car troubles. I was planning to repair my car and then pay my mom back with the money I made at the group home. I was also planning to save my money to get my first book published with this money. I was then planning to learn the value of responsibility while working there as well. I was hoping to build the confidence I needed to attain the woman of my dreams with this responsibility and money. I continued to hold out hope that my car was going to be repaired to continue these plans. Unfortunately, I was learning that this work was not my path to the woman of my dreams.

I hated not having a car. I hated not having the financial means to take care of myself because I was broke. I felt so guilty about having to borrow so much money from my mother for the car. I had to borrow the money for the car repairs and for the car to be towed every time it broke down. So, I was completely self-reliant upon my mother. I did not know what I might have done if my mother had not been there to bail me out both those weekends. Honestly, I do not know how I ever might have survived at all without my parents. My parents were the only reason I had a safe place to eat, sleep, shower, and relax. My two weekends of feeling trapped at this group home helped me to see how truly grateful I was for my parents being around. I was especially grateful for my mother. I was grateful for my mother since she was the only one helping as I lost my car. Alas, I had two nights where I was feeling trapped at this group home.

I had no food and had a very difficult time sleeping that weekend I was trapped at the group home. My nights of sleeping at this group home were so uncomfortable because it was so loud there. It was so loud because the people working there were watching television all night and because of the screaming patients. I had no choice though I had to stay at this group home since I had no car. My only escape was to quit this work at the group home. Yet, I knew quitting was not an option because I needed the money to pay my mother for all the car repairs. Another reason why I knew quitting this work was not an option was because I knew how difficult it was to find work after losing my work at the grocery store and going to the work fair.

My recovery from these financial losses was going to be much more difficult than I thought because I was going to lose my car. The entire time I was calling the mechanic and towing my car I always had this belief that my car was going to be repaired. I never once entertained the thought of losing my car until I made the call to my mechanic that dark Monday.

The Monday when I lost my car started off horribly. I had not eaten. I had not had a shower for three days. So, this alone had me feeling horrible. Then, the supervisor at the group home started the day off with a meeting and it was not a good meeting. The supervisor was yelling at us because there was some missing medication. She did not know the culprit. She wanted to clean house at the group home by firing everyone. So, this meeting and how I was feeling after not showering or eating was already leading to the start of a horrible day. Finally, my mother arrived, and the devastating drive home started. As she was driving me home, I told her about the meeting we had and that I was not sure about still having work. All of this happened before I even started making a call to my mechanic to see if my car had been repaired.

I called my mechanic during the drive home from work. I was still expecting my mechanic to tell me that the car had been repaired and I could get it when we got home. Instead, he told me that the car was unrepairable because I had never gotten an oil change. When I first heard the news of my car being gone, I was shocked from disbelief. I could not believe I was going to be without a car. The loss of my car was devastating because it meant the loss of my freedom. Also, I knew that being without a car meant the loss of my work at the group home because I had to have a car to transport people back and forth. So, after I lost my car, I was devastated. I did not know how to move forward without a car and this work at the group home.

The loss of my car was definitely more devastating than the loss of my employment. This loss was more devastating because I feared losing my freedom and mobility. What I feared the most though was that the loss of my car was going to lead to the loss of the library. I knew that the loss of the library meant the loss of my beautiful blonde library angel. I feared that this loss was the one loss I could not tolerate. This was the one loss I could not tolerate since I feared it might lead to the loss of my passion for writing. These fears of what I might be losing by the loss of my car made my drive home very uncomfortable. Sadly, I also knew my mother was not someone I could go to for support during my drive home either. I knew I was not going to get support from her because I had borrowed so much money from her only to lose my car.

Unfortunately, she was driving me home and I felt I had to tell someone about this shocking loss.

I started to tell her about the call. I told her about how my car was finished and unrepairable. I was right to avoid telling her though because she did not provide me with any type of support. Instead, she was getting angry with me for not changing the oil. I could not deal with my mother blaming me, plus how I was feeling about losing my car and work. So, I had her let me out of the car so that I could walk the rest of the way home after I got a Pepsi. Once I finally got home, I started calling people about the loss of my car. I started by calling the director of the group home to let her know I was not going to have a car anymore. I told her that I did not see how I was going to be able to continue to work at the group home. This obviously did not make her happy especially after the meeting we had right before my drive home. Afterwards, all I could do was sit and wait to hear from the group home if I still had my work with them or not. After calling the director, I called my mechanic to see what I had to do about the car. Thinking about the car was so painful though, that I simply wanted it all to be over. Thus, when he told me he could junk the car I was relieved to hear this, so I told him to junk it.

The final call I made after losing my car was to a support line for Portage Path. The support line did not help. It never helps much to call the support line because to get support from them you have to talk, and this is the last thing that I want to do when I am suffering. So, I made the call and said nothing as I heard them say hello and I disconnected the line. Then, I decided to call Portage Path to see if any one was available for me to talk at the office. They told me that they were sure they could find someone, so I started going to Portage Path to see someone. However, as I was going their for some social support, I discovered I never needed their support.

I discovered my passion for writing was the only support I needed to start to heal from the loss of my car. I started to find the healing power of my passion for writing when I decided to write an email to my supervisor. I sent it during my trip to Portage Path. As I wrote this email, I was able to tell him about what happened with greater detail. Also, I described how I was hoping to resolve the situation. I felt much better after writing this email because when I was writing it, I felt this was a much safer outlet than me getting any social support. Finally, I arrived at Portage Path and I was able to talk to one of the counselors there. After leaving Portage Path, I felt great about finding somewhere safe to voice my thoughts verbally. I believe the email I sent though was my most effective way to heal. Yet, I was not ready to see how truly powerful my passion for writing could be at healing me from the pain of loss. My true power of healing was not going to be felt for another few months. So, for now, I felt Portage Path was what I needed to heal, and I was grateful to them for being there for me to get this social support.

I needed to find a safe place to air out my feelings about my losses without arguing. I knew that I was not going to get the support I needed from my parents. Thus, my choice was to go to Portage Path for support. However, this was one of the last times I was going to go to Portage Path for support unless it was for individual therapy. I was going to discover my passion for writing was a much more effective way to deal with any of my losses after this loss. After seeing my counselor, I went home to try and find a way to move forward after the loss of my car.

My passion for writing and the counselor I saw at Portage Path helped to give me the support I needed to move forward. I was ready to try and move forward after I got this support. When I got home, I found out that I got a call from the supervisor to find out what happened. Then, we both made an appointment to speak about the situation more and I was feeling good about my chance of returning to work there after the call. I was feeling good because he was asking me if I might be willing to work at a new group home that was closer to where I lived. So, I was thinking great my work with the group home might not be lost. I was feeling hopeful for my future again. I thought I was going to continue to make good money and learn responsibility. Then, later that same night I got another call from another place of employment.

This other place of work was to do demos for a grocery store. I did not care about this employment at first because I was feeling so confident about returning to the group home. I soon discovered that this work though was going to be the perfect work for my passion for writing. I had two interviews that I was going to go to that following Friday. I was fairly certain that I was going to return to my work at a group home, so again I did not care much about my interview with Bon Gout. Yet, I was still planning to go to the interview because I could have been wrong about returning to the group homes. Friday arrived, and I went to my interview with Bon Gout at about noon. The interview went well, and I was hired. I accepted the offer because I was still not sure about returning to my work at the group homes. Finally, I had my meeting with them at two and I was looking forward to it since I thought I was returning to work. Then, once the meeting started, I realized that I was actually being fired. Thus, my journey of learning responsibility was over, and I went to work at Bon Gout which was the perfect work for writing.

The Perfect Work For Writing

Bon Gout was going to be the perfect work for writing. I did not have to work many hours and it was decent pay for the hours I did work. I was only scheduled to work about seven hours a day a few days a week. There were some weeks when we might get five days a week during the holiday season. However, most weeks I was only working about four days a week. This was my schedule when it was slow, and these were the hours I liked because it allowed me time to pursue my passion for writing while still making some money. We were scheduled to start work between the hours of ten and eleven. We then got off work sometime between the hours of five and seven. I loved this schedule because it allowed me to get to some of my writing before and after work. Then, the days I had off I could get to even more of my writing.

The fluctuating schedule that we had at Bon Gout was what was making this work the perfect work for my passion for writing. I had several weeks when I was able to get to the bulk of my writing, then other weeks when I could work and save money. This schedule was great because it allowed me to cultivate my passion for writing while also saving for a car. Unfortunately, I started thinking about leaving Bon Gout when I went several weeks without getting that many hours. I was thinking about leaving because I hated not having the freedom that you got from having a car. So, there was no way around it I was going to need to find another place to work if I ever hoped to get a car. Sadly, I knew this meant that I had to leave the perfect work for writing. However, I was not thrilled about leaving my work at Bon Gout when I knew how much I loved working there. I loved the fluctuating schedule that we were getting every week at Bon Gout. Also, I loved how this work was not difficult work to do since all we were doing was handing out samples of food. I even found some of the customers enjoyable to serve because they were such nice people for me to start to socialize with at times. I especially enjoyed listening to this one old man talk about his life as a wood carver. My coworkers were the best part of my work there though because they were such sweet old ladies.

I did not want to leave Bon Gout once I knew that this work was the perfect work for writing. I knew how difficult it was for me to find tolerable work because of my work history. When I think about my work history, I knew that there were not many places that I found tolerable to work at every day. However, there were a few places I tolerated during high school.

I found my work during high school was tolerable because of what was happening with beautiful women. I found these experiences with beautiful women made me forget all about how much I hated work. The first place I ever worked at during high school was going to be this Gyro place within the mall. My work at this Gyro place was tolerable because this was where I was going to get a letter from the beautiful blonde from high school. I could have never gotten this letter though if not for the great manager I worked with there. This manager was very encouraging and supportive. I even remember him having lunch with me sometimes to socialize.

I do not remember that much about my work during high school. I only remember my experiences with beautiful women while I was working there. One of these memories that I have is of this beautiful blonde angel I worked with at this fast-food restaurant. I do not remember much about this coworker other than that she was blonde and beautiful. Instead, most of what I remember about her is how she was flirting with me one night at this fast-food restaurant. I remember her asking me questions about this necklace that I was wearing. I remember her standing really close to me and holding this necklace that was still around my neck at the time. It was a very intimate and unforgettable moment. Sadly though, I did not know what to do after this moment, so I left not knowing what could have happened with her. Honestly, I am not certain what happened with my work at the fast-food restaurant after this intimate moment either.

The second place I worked at where I had a wonderful experience with a beautiful woman was also going to occur while I was attending high school. This wonderful experience was going to happen while I was working at this music store. I do not remember that much about the physical appearance of this beautiful woman. All I remember about her is that she had black hair and that she was a supervisor rather than my coworker. Most of what I remember about this beautiful black haired supervisor was what happened with her. I remember we started talking and I learned she liked Disney miniatures from the Disney Store. So, when I took a break, I went to the Disney Store to buy her a Disney miniature of her favorite character. Then, we started talking some more and even had lunch together. Eventually, this all led to me asking her out to a movie and our first date. Unfortunately, I did not realize that this was a date, so I had her pay. Also, not much happened during the date because of my social anxiety. So, this was not a very successful date obviously. Once we returned to work after our first date, she started flirting with another coworker and she started to shun me at work. This was to eventually lead me to leaving my work at this music store because I was so uncomfortable around her. I do not remember if I was fired or if I simply stopped working there. All I remember is that I had to get away from her. I saw this beautiful black-haired supervisor one more time at a video store. It was a few weeks after leaving the music store and she joked with me about something. However, I could not respond because I lost all hope with beautiful women after the music store.

I lost all hope of ever getting a beautiful woman after I was shunned by this beautiful supervisor at the music store. I forgot about the beautiful black-haired supervisor from the music store until a few nights ago when I started listening to Savage Garden. Once I listened to this album, and I heard the song Truly, Madly, Deeply I was flooded with memories of her. I remembered our date and how she shunned me after our first date.

All these memories of her made me realize that this was the moment when I lost all hope of getting a beautiful woman. Unfortunately, this hope then did not return until I discovered my beautiful blonde library angel.

I did not only lose all hope of ever getting a beautiful woman once I was shunned. I could not tolerate work anymore after losing this hope of getting a beautiful woman as well. I never found any motivation to keep my work after I lost this hope. I continued to go to work because I needed money, however work was all I saw for my future. I saw no light to lead me out of the darkness of having to work. I always thought of the word work as being another synonym for hell and nobody wants to go to hell. I applied for work, got work, tried to keep work, lost work, and then applied again, all because I needed money. Yet, I felt this was a meaningless and hopeless cycle to go through if I had no hope of being with a beautiful woman.

This work cycle that I went through continued even once my beautiful blonde library angel introduced me to my passion for writing. I continued to go to work and lose work. I still was finding it difficult to keep work due to my social anxiety. Yet, what was changing was my view of work. I stopped seeing work as the most important thing within my life. I knew I still had to work to make money because this was the only way that I was going to get the things that I needed or wanted. Working was the only way that I was going to get my book published and marketed. However, I knew that my time was also important because time was my way of cultivating my passion for writing. So, my struggle to find a balance of having both time and money continued. My view of work made work more tolerable since I viewed work differently than other people. This view was helping me to see calling off and losing work as not being so traumatic because I knew whatever work I was doing was temporary. I did not see any work as being tolerable at the start of my spiritual journey. All work was extroverted work, and my debilitating social anxiety was still a part of my life, so I felt I was never going to keep this work.

This was my view of work at the start of my spiritual journey. I did not believe I was ever going to find work I could tolerate and possibly even enjoy. Then, I discovered Bon Gout, and all of this started to change. I knew that I could not stay since I was not making enough money there, yet I did not want to leave either because it was helping me with my social anxiety.

My journey with Bon Gout started the same day I lost my work at a group home. The loss of my work at the group home and the loss of my car was devastating. My fear was that the loss of my car and this work at the group home might lead me into another pit of darkness. However, this never happened because Bon Gout called the same day as these two losses. I also had my passion for writing to help me deal with these losses. My passion for writing helped me to get a better view of what these two losses meant for my future. It helped me to see that my time was going to be best spent cultivating my passion for writing rather than working every day.

I created this new view through the help of my passion for writing. My time spent writing helped me to see that I was lucky to have this work at Bon Gout. It helped me to see that even though I was not making as much money there, at least I was still making some money. Bon Gout also helped me to see that by already having this work I could spend more of my time writing. So, I was starting to see the loss of my work at the group home was a good thing since it gave me more time to write. Another reason why losing this work was a good thing was because I got rid of the anxiety I was feeling about working there. I was feeling this anxiety because I never felt the path of responsibility was the right path for me to follow. I always felt this was the path other people wanted me to follow since it made you a better person. However, I still did not agree with this view of responsibility. I still viewed responsibility as something that made you more miserable since it kept you from doing what you loved. This view that I had of being responsible plus my view of the importance of time changed the way I viewed these two losses. I started to view the loss of my work at the group home, and even the loss of my car, as a good thing since these two losses were going to allow me more time to cultivate my writing every day.

It took me about a month to start my work at Bon Gout because of all the computer training. This time allowed me more time to cultivate and strengthen my passion for writing. I had my first book completed and was feeling confident about what I had written. However, I was still having doubts about the direction and flow of my first book. These doubts led me to starting over from scratch because I felt I could do better. I started to rewrite my first book around February of 2017. The one thing I never doubted was the title. I was still going to call it *The Beautiful Blonde Library Angel*. However, this was the only thing that remained the same. It took me most of 2017 to rewrite my first book. Once I completed it, I had written twenty chapters. Each chapter consisted of twenty pages, and the entire book was four hundred pages.

My first day of work at Bon Gout arrived. I was working where my mother worked. This did not help my social anxiety because I felt as if I was representing her as well. This made me feel more trapped by work because if I left, she was going to be affected by this as well. Thus, the night before work I was very anxious about going to work because I knew that it was going to involve me talking to customers every time that I told them about the samples. I spent most of the night before work watching videos and researching how to deal with my social anxiety. Finally, after two hours of research, I got to sleep. Then, I awoke, and I went to work.

Bon Gout was one of my favorite places to work because of my coworkers. My coworkers were some of the friendliest old ladies that I had ever been around. It took me a few weeks to feel socially comfortable around them. Then, once I started talking, I never wanted to stop talking to them. I enjoyed talking to them so much because they reminded me of my grandmothers. So, I started to refer to these sweet old coworkers as my wise old grandmothers.

It was not until one of the kindest old grandmothers started to talk to me that I felt comfortable around them. This wise old grandmother had a very inviting way of speaking to me which led me to feel less guarded. Then, she started to invite me to have lunch with her which caused me a great deal of anxiety at first. However, gradually my anxiety started to pass, and I was able to talk to her about things I had never spoken to people about before. I was able to talk to her about my social anxiety. I was able to talk to her about my parents. I was able to talk to her about "My Wonderful French Childhood". Mostly though, I was able to talk to her about the book I was writing. These lunches with this sweet old grandmother led me to start talking to some of the other wise old grandmothers. Eventually, I was able to talk to several grandmothers.

It got to a point where I was socially comfortable around ten of these old wise grandmothers. I even started to consider four of them the golden girls of work because they reminded me of the old ladies from *The Golden Girls*. Each one reminded me of Dorothy, Sophia, and Blanche. Then, the sweet old grandmother who introduced me to them all reminded me of Rose. The more time I spent at Bon Gout the more I found myself talking to some of the other coworkers there as well. Socializing with everyone at this grocery store helped me gain some confidence. I hoped socializing at work might even lead me to socializing outside of work.

I wanted to learn to socialize more. I was hoping my work at Bon Gout was going to help me to start to learn the social skills to socialize with people. However, I was going to have a difficult time remaining at Bon Gout for several reasons. One reason why I had trouble remaining there was because it was difficult for me to remain at one employer without leaving. I had grown accustomed to jumping from work to work. So, staying at one place was difficult. Also, I found I was focusing more upon the negatives there. I was unable to focus upon the relationships I was building with the wise old grandmothers. Instead, I was thinking about not getting enough hours. I was thinking about never getting a raise at work. I was thinking about never being able to get any benefits. Mostly though, I thought about how I disliked the manager.

I thought this manager was one of the worst managers I was ever going to have until I started my work at a grocery store. All of these reasons were why I was starting to look for work elsewhere. I had my mind set upon leaving, so I was looking for any opportunity to do so. However, I was not very motivated to find other work because I still did like working with my coworkers and talking to them, so I was only applying for work once or twice a week. I was only applying to places that felt like they were an improvement to this work. Eventually, my time of applying for work led me to an interview with a nearby grocery store. This was a grocery store that I had always wanted to work at, so I was thinking this might be better work.

I thought working at this grocery store was going to lead to a better future since it was unionized. I thought this could be a place where I could grow if I could do well there. I knew I was taking a pay cut by going there. However, I thought over time I could get better pay with raises which was something I could not get at Bon Gout. So, I was excited about my future at this grocery store when I started to work there. Sadly, I learned this excitement was misguided when I got there. So, I learned a valuable lesson once I left Bon Gout for this grocery store. The valuable lesson I learned was to listen to my gut instincts. My gut instincts were telling me to remain at Bon Gout. However, I decided to ignore all of these signs and I decided to leave anyways. I felt confident about this decision at the time since I felt I could have a future there.

I started my work at this grocery store the fourth of July. I started out my first day of work at this grocery store full of hope and confidence. I was looking forward to starting a new prosperous career at this grocery store. I knew I was going to be taking a pay cut by working there and I was sacrificing the social growth I had made at Bon Gout. However, I thought it was all going to be worth it because I saw myself growing as I worked at the grocery store. Then, my first day started and I was ready to make a good impression. I was looking forward to the opportunities I thought I was going to have at this grocery store. Also, I was excited by all the beautiful young women that I saw as I first got to work. All these young women were working at the front of the store, so I was looking forward to any opportunity I had to pass by them. So, my first day at this grocery store was not off to a bad start. Then, this hope and confidence that I was feeling started to fade away every time I had to talk to someone at work.

I was starting to learn that working at this grocery store was much like attending high school. This was going to make it difficult for me to feel socially comfortable. It was this social discomfort that was going to lead me to losing my work at this grocery store. A part of the reason why I felt so uncomfortable there was because I was so socially spoiled at Bon Gout. I never spoke to anyone at this grocery store until my final week there. Also, they never trained me much, instead they complained about me to the manager about my mistakes and being slow. Apparently, this was how things were run at this grocery store and I could not adapt to this environment. I knew that it started from the top though, I knew it started with the store manager.

I hated everything about my manager at this grocery store. I could not stand to be anywhere near him because he was relentlessly finding fault with my work. I was never able to do right by him. It all started with him calling me to the office to tell me that I was not doing well, and I needed to start to work faster. I thought I was doing well at the grocery store before this first meeting. Then, he found fault with me not knowing things at work and how I spoke to the customers there. The more time I spent at this grocery store, the more I regretted leaving my work as a demo person at Bon Gout. I hated my work at the grocery store because of the manager and the atmosphere. Yet, I still had to make money, so I continued to go to work there.

I lost all respect for the manager at this grocery store because he was such a horrible person. He even reminded me of Hitler because of how he walked around the store. He even had a Hitler mustache. Once I lost all respect for the manager, I returned to my old ways of work. I read books at work and I left work while still getting paid. This was how I showed my disrespect for how businesses tried to take advantage of their employees. Finally, my ninety days were over, and I was fired from this grocery store. The manager did not even have the backbone to fire me himself, instead his assistant manager did it while he took a vacation. After I was fired, I learned that other people were treated horribly by this manager as well. So, I was happy when I was fired because it meant never having to deal with him again. I never had to deal with someone who gained so much pride from making other people so miserable. The cruelty other people enact upon other people is something that I will never be able to understand.

There was not much about my work at this grocery store that I enjoyed. I enjoyed the work itself that I had to do while I was there because it was a distraction from my social anxiety. Also, I never got tired of looking at all the beautiful young angels at the front of the store. However, the atmosphere at this grocery was changing what I thought about them. I stopped seeing them as sweet young beautiful angels. Instead, I was seeing them as these preppy and snobby girls who were only after men with money or looks. I spent most of my time at this grocery store regretting leaving my work as a demo person at Bon Gout. So, I was trying to return. I started applying as soon as my regrets about leaving started. Unfortunately, the manager from Bon Gout was not going to let me return. This manager never cared for me that much because I was not following the rules when I worked there. Also, she hated that I never worked when she needed me to work during my days off. Thus, I was gradually starting to realize that I might never find my way back to Bon Gout and the perfect work for my writing.

The Power to Heal

I started to discover that my passion for writing had the power to heal after I lost my work at this grocery store. My passion for writing was going to help me see that losing my work at this grocery store was more of a blessing than a curse since I hated working there so much. Sure, I was going to miss the pay and the beautiful angels working there. The one thing I definitely did not miss though was how this narcistic boss treated his workers like his minions.

I started walking to the library after I was fired from this grocery store. It only took fifteen minutes for me to get to the library. As I was walking to the library, I thought about how I was going to miss the weekly paychecks that I got from this grocery store, yet not the work. Finally, I arrived at the library and I started to reapply for work at Bon Gout since I was still hoping to find a way to return. I spent the rest of my time at the library writing about this loss.

My passion for writing gave me the power to heal from the loss of my work at the grocery store. This power to heal was also going to help me get over another devastating loss. My passion for writing was also going to give me the power to heal from the pain and disappointment of being rejected by one of the library angels that I thought might be interested.

Annabelle 2 was the beautiful library angel that I was going to try and approach with a letter. I still did not think that I had a real chance with her or any of the other beautiful angels. I knew that these beautiful angels were still half my age and probably way out of my league. However, my gut instincts told me that I had to try and find out the truth because she might be interested. I thought she might be interested because of how she was smiling and looking at me when I was looking at her. Then, I saw her looking and smiling at me as she was walking by me one day as I was about ready to leave and I felt the urge to find out if I had a chance with her. Usually, I ignored my urges to do something. However, this time I could not ignore these urges.

This time I had to do something when I felt there were signs of interest. I still did not really believe I had a chance with her. However, I had to try to see if I might be wrong. I had to see if I had a chance with her. So, I started writing her a poem inspired by the moment and by her beauty. I called the poem Ode to Annabelle 2. It was not a bad poem for my first poem, although I decided not to give it to her because it was too much for my first approach. So, instead, I decided to write her a letter to tell her how I felt since I still could not verbally tell her.

I knew I was never going to be able to approach her if it meant talking to her. I knew socializing was not my path to success since I still lacked the confidence to say anything to her. I knew my passion for writing was my only way of finding success with her or any beautiful woman. So, I knew that socializing was never going to be my way of attaining any of my beautiful angels. I thought my only path to success with them was if I wrote down my feelings.

I had the idea of writing her a letter while I was walking home from the library. However, this was not the first time I thought of writing her a letter. The first time I thought of writing her this letter was seven months ago while I was walking home from the library. Unfortunately, I never wrote her a letter back then since I lacked the confidence to give it to her.

I could not stop thinking about giving her the letter. I knew I had to try and find the confidence to give it to her. I did not care what anyone else thought as I was walking toward her. I did not care since I had to know the truth. I also did not care that it was only four o'clock, so she had to work for another four hours once I gave it to her. I knew this could mean me sitting with these feelings of rejection if she did not accept the letter. Yet, I did not care because I simply had to know the truth. So, Monday October 2nd, 2017 at four o'clock I finally found out.

I spent a week preparing the letter for her. I was ready to see if any of the hopes and dreams I had of having a relationship with her were real. I finally found the confidence to see if I had any chance with her. I blocked out all excuses I thought of to not find out the truth. I feared I might never find this confidence again. Finally, I started walking toward Annabelle 2.

My stomach was nauseated. My hands were clammy. I could not stop trembling and shaking from all the anxiety that I was feeling about giving her the letter. I felt as if everyone at the library was watching my every move as I was walking toward her. However, I did not care because I had to find out the truth. I refused to allow my anxiety or anything else stop me from finding out the truth about whether I had a chance with Annabelle 2 or not. I knew that not knowing was going to be much worse than confronting my anxiety. Finally, the moment arrived, and I had to say something. I told her I had written her a letter and then I asked her if she was willing to accept it. She told me no. Alas, the pain and disappointment of being rejected started.

The pain and disappointment of my rejection started with me thinking I might have a chance with Annabelle 2. Annabelle 2 was the only library angel I ever thought I might possibly have the slightest chance with since the others were too out of reach and out of my league. I never really thought I had a real chance with her either, however I felt I had to find out the truth.

I spent the week thinking about how to give her the letter and writing it. I was also coping with all the fear and anxiety about how to give it to her. I was talking to my therapist and my father about the letter I was hoping to give to her. I was going to the library to write and rewrite the letter I was hoping to give to her. I was spending all this time preparing for the world of opportunities that I was hoping might develop after giving her the letter. Sadly, all of this preparation was going to be for nothing because she was going to reject my letter. I was devastated after she rejected my letter. I thought her rejecting my letter was the second worst thing that could happen. The worst thing that could happen was still me never finding the confidence to give it to her at all. Her rejecting my letter meant that my hopes and dreams of having a future with her were over before they even started. I was not sure how to deal with Annabelle 2's rejection. However, I knew I was going to have to find a way to move forward.

It took everything I had to merely get back to my seat after her rejection. Once there I was unable to move and I did not know how I was going to ever move again. What was going to make this rejection so devastating was that I felt so much hope before she rejected my letter. Before she rejected my letter, I had a day when I went to the movies and had this moment of pure joy. This moment of pure joy started with me going to the movies thinking about the future I was hoping to have with Annabelle 2. This moment of pure joy was created by me imagining what might happen once she read the letter. I started to imagine that after she read the letter, she might call me, and this might lead to us talking for several hours. Then, I imagined how this might lead to us having our first few dates. Finally, I imagined having this relationship with her.

Dating and having a relationship was something I could only imagine having with a beautiful woman. I never knew what it was like to feel the kindness and warmth of a beautiful woman. The only thing I have ever known about beautiful women is their beauty and my obsession with their beauty. So, as I started walking toward her, I had no idea what might happen if she actually accepted the letter. I could only imagine what I was hoping might happen. My imagined relationship even went to us getting married someday and having a family. I was imagining having someone who actually wanted to spend time with me voluntarily. Most importantly, I was imagining having someone who I could even talk to and be vulnerable around.

Imagining this relationship was giving me the confidence to find out the truth about Annabelle 2. I could not believe I was planning to give her this letter and find out the truth after obsessing over her for a year. Yet, I knew I had to see if there was any way this imagined life could be real life. This imaginary relationship was giving me hope, and I did not want to lose it. I wanted to keep this hope alive for as much time as possible. Especially since, I felt so much hope the week before I finally tried to give Annabelle 2 the letter to see if she may be interested.

I had this moment of pure joy the Thursday before I went to find out the truth. This moment of pure joy led me to writing the letter for Annabelle 2. Then, that following Friday, I spent the entire day writing her the letter. My plans were to write the letter all day Friday and then Saturday I was going to find a way to build my confidence so that I could give her the letter. I thought that these were some great plans. Unfortunately, my plans had not gone accordingly. I spent the entire day Friday writing and preparing the letter as planned. Then, I was hoping to give it to her that following Saturday. However, my plans were then interrupted by Annabelle 2.

Annabelle 2 was putting some books away right beside me at the library. This was causing me a great deal of anxiety. It caused me anxiety since I wanted to give the letter to her at that moment. The problem was that I had nothing ready to give to her. I was still rewriting the letter I hoped to give to her. I knew I still had to print it out and get the envelope ready before I was ready to give it to her. So, I was going back and forth about whether to give it to her or not. Finally, I decided that I had to say something to her. However, I did not walk toward her to give her the letter, instead I asked her if she was going to be at the library that following Saturday. She told me that she was going to be working from one to five. Then, she asked me why I wanted to know, and I could not think of a response because of my debilitating social anxiety.

I was frozen and silent. I had trouble simply getting back to my chair which was only about a few steps away from where I was standing. I was shaking so much from my anxiety that I had trouble walking even a few steps though, then I finally got to my seat. Once I got back to my seat though, I was thinking twice about giving Annabelle 2 the letter that Saturday. I was thinking how I might have made her uncomfortable by trying to find out her hours Friday. Thus, I turned to the only coping mechanism I knew of to deal with the anxiety I was feeling. I turned to my passion for writing. My passion for writing helped to decrease my anxiety and once I felt better, I thought about apologizing to her before leaving the library. I told her the reason I wanted to know when she was working was because I wanted to give her something. Looking back, I am not sure if my apologizing to her helped that much. I think my apology could have actually hurt my chances with her since it may have made her even more uncomfortable. However, it helped to build my confidence so I could think about giving her the letter once more.

I started walking home thinking about how I was going find the confidence to finally learn the truth about Annabelle 2. I knew I was going to have to say something to her if I gave her the letter. I knew I could not simply give her a letter without saying a word. Finally, it was Saturday September 30th, 2017. The day of the approach had arrived. I was walking to the library thinking about what I was going to say. Finally, I got to the library at around ten o'clock.

I started out my day at the library listening to Enrique Iglesias. This was going be the theme music that was going to inspire me to finally give Annabelle 2 the letter. I spent the first few hours at the library reviewing and editing the letter I was hoping to give her. I went to Mamouth to get some envelopes so that I could write Annabelle 2 upon one of them. Then, when I returned to the library, I printed the letter and put it into an envelope. Finally, all I had left to do was give her the letter once I saw her. I tried to get back to my writing while I was waiting to see her. However, my social anxiety was not allowing me to think about anything else other than giving her the letter. So, instead of my writing, I started to message my friend from Florida about what I was thinking. As the hours passed, I noticed she was nowhere to be seen. So, I realized I was not going to be able to give her the letter since she already left. I was thinking she switched her hours because I had made her so uncomfortable that previous Friday.

I finally left the library at about four. I felt I lost all hope of having a chance with Annabelle 2 after leaving the library that Saturday. I walked home knowing there was nothing I could do about it until Monday. I could not stop thinking about how I might have ruined any chance I had with her by approaching her that previous Friday. I also feared that I might have ruined my chances with another library angel by approaching her that previous Friday. The letter for Annabelle 2 did not have her name within the letter. It was only describing her as a beautiful brunette and the beautiful Irish library angel was also a beautiful brunette. So, had I not asked about her hours, I could have given the letter to the beautiful Irish angel instead that Saturday. Unfortunately, since I had approached Annabelle 2 that previous Friday, I feared I ruined all of my chances with both library angels. So, I left the library feeling depressed. As I started walking home, I was questioning whether I was ever going to be able to approach Annabelle 2.

I was not thinking about Annabelle 2 the rest of the weekend because my mom told me Florida was not going to happen. My parents were planning to go to Florida because they knew that my grandfather did not have much more time upon this earth. So, my mom wanted to see him one last time before he passed away. This was something I was excited about because it meant that I was going to have the house to myself. This was a part of the reason why I had the confidence to find out the truth about Annabelle 2. I thought that if she did turn me down or reject my letter then I was going to be able to take a break from the library by staying home. Sadly, once I got home, I learned that they were not going to Florida anymore because my father was not ready. My mother was furious that he was not ready, and I was not happy since it meant the loss of my freedom from my parents for a week. I knew I was never going to move out of my parents' home because of my social anxiety and my inability to keep work. So, the only freedom I ever got from them was when they went to see the rest of the family for a few weeks.

The day I was going to approach Annabelle 2 had finally arrived. I started out this Monday by going to see my therapist before I went to the library to see Annabelle 2. I was not too excited about seeing him because I thought he might convince me to not give her the letter. Seeing my therapist was one of the main reasons I wanted to give her the letter Saturday. I was hoping to see my therapist about the disappointment of being rejected rather than for approval. I think I was always expecting to be rejected by Annabelle 2. So, I was preparing to deal with the rejection by seeing my therapist and then I was going to take a break from the library. Sadly, this did not happen. Instead, he supported me approaching her to give her the letter I wrote her.

I repeated what I did Saturday when I finally got to the library. I started out the day listening to Enrique Iglesias as I got ready to give her the letter when she finally started her shift. Finally, I found out the truth Monday October 2nd, 2017. So, there I was sitting at the library frozen from the pain and disappointment of being rejected. I knew that I was going to have to find a way to move forward. So, I turned to my passion for writing to start to heal from the pain and disappointment of her rejection. I wrote about this pain and the disappointment. I wrote about the reasons why I might have been rejected. It could have been that I was too old for her. It could have been that she had a boyfriend. It could have been that she did not find me attractive. It could have been that I never spoke to her. I hated not knowing why I was rejected.

I learned to let go of my need to know the reason why I had been rejected. I learned to redirect my focus to moving forward from the pain and disappointment of this rejection. I turned to my passion for writing as a way to move forward. My passion for writing was going to lead me towards its true power which was its power to heal. After she rejected my letter, I turned to my writing as a source of comfort. Writing was the one thing I could still turn to for comfort. When I was feeling hurt, I wrote. When I was feeling lonely, I wrote. When I was feeling weak, I wrote. Finally, when I was feeling rejected, I wrote as a way to heal from the pain and disappointment of being rejected. Before I started writing though, I had to move to another part of the library. I was not comfortable where I was sitting because I was worried people could look over my shoulders and read my writings. I was not ready for my thoughts to go public because during the writing process I felt very vulnerable. Then, once I completed my writings, I was ready to allow people to see and discuss my writings. However, not during the writing process itself. So, I had to move to feel more comfortable before I could start the writing process. This meant confronting my social anxiety because I needed to walk through the library.

I started to discover the power of healing from my passion for writing by exploring why the rejection hurt so much. I knew it was partly due to the loss of the dream I had of what might have been with Annabelle 2. I was tired of living a life alone. So, I decided to try and give her the letter because I felt I had nothing to lose. I made a choice to choose hope over the belief that I always had of having no chance with her. This choice led me to having a week where I was feeling hopeful about my future. Hope alone made giving her the letter worthwhile.

The downside to feeling this hope was that I risked feeling the pain and disappointment of rejection.

How was I going to move forward from the darkness I was feeling from the pain and disappointment of rejection? I was going to move forward with the one thing that I knew I could always rely upon within my life. I was going to move forward with my passion for writing. My passion for writing helped me find some strength from the pain and disappointment of rejection. I started to discover the power of healing from my passion for writing as soon as I started to explore my feelings with my passion for writing. Once I found a good place to sit with my back to the wall, I spent two hours writing. The more I wrote, the more I felt the true power of my passion for writing. I felt its true power with its ability to help me to heal from being rejected by Annabelle 2. I could not take my eyes off my computer as I sat their writing for two hours. I could not even take my eyes off the computer screen to look at my beautiful blonde library angel.

Two hours had passed. I wrote five pages during these two hours about the pain and disappointment of being rejected. This was when I was introduced to the power of healing from my passion for writing. Sadly, this power of healing was only going to be felt within my world of isolation. Once, I left my world of isolation, I felt the pain and disappointment of being rejected by Annabelle 2 all over again. I felt it all over again as I was leaving the library. However, my passion for writing was able to help me find the strength to at least leave the library. After I left the library, I found out my parents were once again going to go to Florida. So, I was still going to get my break from the library. Then, my father fell as he was going to bed. When I went to tell my mom, I feared that this might mean them not going again. However, my mom still wanted to go, so she started making some calls to make the trip herself.

My father had fallen so much over the past two years of his life that he had great difficulty leaving his spot within the garage. These falls led to his gradual demise. His gradual demise was the second devastating loss to help me see how my writing had the power to heal. Before I dealt with this loss though, I had to deal with the loss of being rejected by Annabelle 2.

My mom was going to be leaving for Florida to see my grandfather that Thursday. I planned to spend Tuesday and Wednesday at the library before she left. I wanted to spend these two days at the library to see if the magic of the library could still be felt. I was going to find that the magic of the library could still be felt because of my beautiful blonde library angel. I still felt I needed a break from the library though after I saw Annabelle 2. I still needed a break because the pain and disappointment of being rejected by her returned after I saw her. So, I needed this break from the library to strengthen my passion for writing and to be with my father.

The Death Of My Father

The death of my father was the second devastating loss that helped me discover the power my passion for writing had to heal. The pain and disappoint of rejection that I felt with Annabelle 2 was my introduction to its power to heal. I started to feel how my passion for writing had the power to heal during my two hours of writing after she rejected my letter. Unfortunately, it was not going to be until the death of my father that I learned of its true power.

My father was my best friend. He was the one person I had left that I could socialize with about anything at any time. My father was very similar to my French Grandmother because they were both great socializers. I always believed that this was the greatest quality any person could possess because of my debilitating social anxiety. This quality made me feel comfortable talking to both of them about almost anything at any time. Unfortunately, I lost my French grandmother soon after returning from France after high school. After losing my grandmother, I still had my best friend to talk to until I moved to Ohio. Then, once I moved to Ohio the only person that I had left to feel socially comfortable around other than my therapists was my father.

The great thing about talking to my father was that I did not have the same barriers as I did with my therapists. I could speak French with my father which was not an option with any of my therapists. Unfortunately, we rarely spoke French because we were so accustomed to speaking English all the time. Another barrier that did not exist with my father was that when I spoke to him there was no time limit, I could talk to him for a few minutes or several hours. This allowed me to feel comfortable talking to him about almost anything at any time. I was able to talk to my father about my history of never having had a girlfriend because he knew all about it. Plus, I was able to talk to him about my obsession with the beautiful blonde library angel. I could talk him about how this library angel introduced me to my passion for writing. I was even able to talk to him about how much I hated work since it made me so miserable. There was nothing that I felt was off limits when I went to talk to my father at his spot within the garage.

I felt so socially comfortable around my father because I never had to worry about him judging me for what I was thinking. One reason why I never worried about him judging me was because I felt superior to him. I felt superior to him because he was always drinking and watching television at his spot within the garage. He rarely left the house to do anything and I knew I was at least leaving the house to try to do something with my life. This feeling of superiority may not have been fair or even accurate since he was the reason, we had a home. However, this was how I felt, and it was a major part of the reason why I felt so comfortable around him. This feeling of superiority allowed me to lose my social anxiety when I was around him. Thus, allowing me to have at least one person to go to for social support. Sadly, I was going to lose my father as this source of social comfort, and it was going to be a devastating loss.

My father and I may not have always agreed with each other about the things we discussed. These disagreements often led to many heated arguments and moments of silence that could last hours or days. When we had these moments of silence, I felt like my father was my worst enemy and I never planned to talk to him again. However, these moments of silence always passed because I knew how important my father was to my social life. Also, my father was always someone to never hold a grudge. This might have had to do with him being French because I believe that French people were very expressive about their emotions. Then, I guess they also knew how to let go of their anger once they were able to express it. I knew from my many years of therapy that the best way to deal with conflict was to air it out by talking about it. I did not really agree with this being the best way to handle conflict with my father though because I feared losing him as the one person that I was socially comfortable around by doing so.

Most of the time our conversations only lasted about five minutes. I learned to avoid certain subjects because they might lead to our heated arguments and moments of silence. I did not like these moments of silence because I hated losing the social comfort, I felt around him. I loved that I could talk to him about anything at anytime. So, I always felt the risk was worth the reward and I kept going back to talk to him at his spot within the garage. I always knew where to find my father when I wanted to talk to him. My father's place was always only a few steps away from where we took off our shoes to go into the house and leave the house. There were days when this was the only time I spoke to my father or anyone else for that matter. So, I suppose it was only right that this was going to be the last spot I was going to ever see him alive.

My father loved sitting at his spot within the garage because he had everything that he cared about at his spot. He had a television to watch the news and sports all day. This was about all he ever watched except late at night he liked to watch Lifetime movies. He had his beer right near him because he sat only a few steps away from the fridge we had downstairs. He also had pen and paper to write when he was thinking and needed some way to express his thoughts. Usually, the things he thought about were money and how much he hated his life. Finally, he was close to being outdoors which was something my father always loved. My father loved being outdoors whether it was cold or hot. However, he always preferred the heat over the cold.

My father loved the heat, and he hated the cold. This was something I could never understand about him. I could never understand how he enjoyed the sweat and discomfort that went with always being hot. Another thing I could never understand was how he could love gardening so much. My father always loved to garden when he was able to physically do some gardening. He loved to be outdoors, and this was something I could never understand since I preferred being indoors.

This love for being outdoors was also something he inherited from my French grandmother. These two traits which he inherited from her were what helped me to remember my French grandmother. Yet, his social skills were what I truly treasured about him.

The death of my father was a devastating loss because it meant I was losing my best friend and my last connection to "My Wonderful French Childhood". After returning from my trip to France after high school, I learned everyone I was close to from France was gone. My French grandparents were both dead. My French soulmate Annabelle got married. Around this same time, I also sadly learned that Pierre-Yves committed suicide. Again, Pierre-Yves was my favorite French cousin and one of my best friends. So, my father was the only person left from "My Wonderful French Childhood. Thus, the death of my father, not only meant that I was losing my best friend, I had also lost my last connection to "My Wonderful French Childhood."

This loss was not so devastating though since I knew that my memories of "My Wonderful French Childhood" were going to remain alive with my passion for writing. I learned more about the power of my passion for writing after the death of my father. I was learning more about its power since the more time I had to write, the more memories I uncovered. Uncovering all of these memories, was helping me to heal from the devastating loss of my father.

One of these great memories that I had of my father was of a road trip we took to visit some French castles. This was a memory I always loved having of my father because it was of a time when my father was truly my best friend. We took this road trip together during the last year of "My Wonderful French Childhood". During this road trip, my father and I had some of the best conversations of our lives. Most of these conversations were about his marriage to my mother and why he could not divorce her. I learned a great deal about my father during these conversations and I never felt closer to him then I did during these conversations. These conversations and this road trip I took with him were going to be the best memories I had of him.

My father was both my best friend and my worst enemy. I may not have had the best relationship with my father. However, my father was almost always there for me to talk to when I needed some social support.

This was so important to someone with social anxiety. So, the day I lost my father was scary because I feared never talking to anyone else again. I was already closed off and alone before my father's passing. So, after he passed away, I had no friends or family to go to for social support. I tried to get social support from my wise old grandmothers, however I could not verbally express myself to get their support. I was simply incapable of dealing with both my social anxiety and the sadness I felt from his loss to get any social support.

My break from the library changed the way I thought about pursuing my passion for writing. It also gave me some quality time with my father before he passed away. I was going to start my days cleaning and cooking. Around noon, I had lunch and watched some television. Then, I spent about five hours doing some writing and researching how to get published. This was when I discovered an article by Stephen King that changed my way of thinking. This article was very enlightening, and one statement stood out above the rest. This statement that stood out was that Stephen King wrote ten pages a day. After I read this, I realized that I was not writing enough because I was only writing about one or two pages a day. I knew that I could write more.

I started thinking about how I could change my lifestyle to be a better writer. I was prepared to make some serious changes to be a more passionate writer. I started making these changes by rearranging my room, so I had a place to write, watch TV, sleep, and meditate. Meditation was something I felt was important because it helped me to deal with my social anxiety when I had to reenter reality. So, I took breaks from trying to meditate every day, yet I always retuned to it eventually. After rearranging my room, I started to clear out and then reorganize my computer files. Then, I spent a week cleaning the house to not have cleaning stop me from writing ten pages a day. Finally, I started making plans for how I was going to make changes to the way I was living so that I could start writing ten pages a day. All of these changes were from me reading that one statement from a Stephen King article. Once my break was over, I was ready to start pursuing the changes to my life I planned out. However, all my lifestyle changes were going to be interrupted by the grief I was going to feel from the loss of my father.

My mom returned from Florida and my break from the library was over. I was now ready to start living out the plans I had made for my new life as a passionate writer. I needed this break to deal with the pain and disappointment of being rejected by Annabelle 2. This break helped me to heal from this rejection and I was ready to return to the magic of the library. More importantly, I wanted to return to my passion for writing and my beautiful blonde library angel. Sadly, I was soon going to learn that life had other plans when these plans of pursuing my passion for writing to be a more passionate writer were disrupted by another more devasting loss.

It was Saturday October 14th, 2017 when I found my father unconscious at his spot within the garage. It was around ten when I walked into the garage to find him unconscious. His head was laying against the brick wall and he was not moving. I called out to my father several times and there was no response. I saw that his eyes were still moving though and that he was still breathing. So, I thought that somehow, he might magically be alright if I left him alone. Then, my mother walked into the garage and saw that my father was not moving. Neither one of us knew what to do as we saw him there, so she asked if I still wanted to go to get my glasses. I knew that the best thing to do was to call an ambulance, yet I still went for my glasses. I think I chose to go for my glasses because I was still hoping that he might be alright if I left him alone. However, this was a decision that I was going to regret for the rest of my life because when I returned home I found that the garage door was still closed and I knew that my father was dead.

I entered the garage to see if he might still be alive and if this gut feeling I had was wrong. I checked his pulse and his breathing and when I touched him, he was cold as ice. So, I knew he was dead. Once I learned he was dead, I called 911 and the paramedics got there an hour later. I answered all their questions, then they started to explain what was going to happen. They told me that a cop was going to be stationed outside since it was considered a crime scene. Then, I waited for the medical examiner to arrive so that he could investigate the crime scene. The medical examiner did not arrive until two hours later. Then, he started asking me questions. He was making me very uncomfortable with his questions. I started to feel it was more of an interrogation, and this was causing me to get very defensive and made me start arguing with him.

I believe that a part of the reason why I was getting so defensive with him was that I wanted to feel something other than the numbness that I was feeling from the death of my father. My father passed away and I was simply going through the motions. This anger that I was feeling when I was arguing with the examiner was the first real emotion that I felt. Eventually, I started to calm down and I was able to answer his questions to get him to leave. After I answered his questions, I apologized for arguing with him since I felt the need to do so. Then before he left, he started explaining the rest of the process for the death of my father. He was going to remove the body for the autopsy. Then, we were going to have to wait for a few days to hear the results. As we waited, we had to choose a funeral home for cremating my father. This was the last time I was going to have to physically deal with his death. We did have a memorial dinner for him during Thanksgiving. However, by that time, I already started the grieving process. I started the grieving process the moment that I had the house to myself to start writing.

The medical examiner took my father for an autopsy and my mother went to talk to a family member for support. So, I had the house all to myself. Finally, I was able to turn to my passion for writing to start the healing process. One thing that bothered me about my best friend's death was that I never cried or even got depressed. I felt a great deal of anxiety and fear about his passing because I thought I might never find someone to talk to again. However, I never did get sad about his death. The reason why I think I never felt that sad about his passing was because my life of never having a girlfriend has led me to living life numb to pain. I feel this numbness because there is no greater sadness than living your life alone. Yet, my inability to feel sadness about the death of my father did not mean that I was not grieving his loss. It only meant that I could not express my grief over his loss with words or emotions. Instead, I was turning to my passion for writing as a way to get over the loss of my father after he passed away.

My passion for writing was my way of healing from the loss of my best friend. The death of my father was going to lead me to finding the true strength of my passion for writing. I knew that socially I was unable to get the support that I needed because of my social anxiety. Hence, it was not until I had the house to myself that I could finally start the process of healing.

I started the process of healing by writing about everything that happened the day my father passed away. I wrote about finding him at his spot within the garage. I wrote about how I was being questioned by the paramedics and the medical examiner. I spent both Saturday and Sunday writing about what happened the day he passed away. Then, I deleted all that I wrote and started over with the healing process that following Monday. So, it was not until that following Monday that I was going to find the real power that my passion for writing had to heal.

I wrote seventy pages about the death of my father that week including the ten pages I deleted that first Sunday. I was writing ten pages a day. I started writing about everything that happened the day of his death again. I wrote about how my father was the one person who understood me best because he was my best friend. I wrote about how he was not a perfect man, yet he was someone I loved a great deal. I wrote about why he was both my best friend and my worst enemy. Finally, I wrote about the fear and anxiety I felt after the death of my father. Fear and anxiety were the emotions I felt the most after his passing. I doubted I was ever going to find someone I could talk to like my father. These were most of the thoughts I was having after his death. Most of these thoughts were very dark and scary thoughts because his loss had me going to a very dark place. I felt my passion for writing was my only way out of this dark place.

I did try to find some social support during my time of grief. I tried to get some social support from the wise old grandmothers working at Bon Gout. However, I was not able to deal with being interrupted by customers all the time. I was never good at talking to people while being interrupted every time a customer wanted to try a sample of food. Also, I was not feeling very comfortable talking to them when there were so many people around me at the store. So, talking to them was not helping. I went to talk to my therapists for support and this was more effective. Unfortunately, it only helped for the hour I was able to see them. The moment I left therapy my feelings of fear and anxiety returned, and I needed to find my support elsewhere. I wanted to talk to my best friend when I got home. Sadly, I knew this was not a viable option since he was not a part of this earth anymore. So, I turned to the only type of support I had left.

I turned to my passion for writing for support as I was grieving over the death of my father. My passion for writing was the one thing I was always able to turn to for support and it was available anytime I needed it. It was available 24/7. I never had to worry about being interrupted when I was writing because it took place within my world of isolation. The best part of my writing though was that I felt my father's presence while I was writing. There were times while writing that I even felt as if my father was still sitting at his spot within the garage. Unfortunately, whenever I returned to reality and went to the garage the pain of his loss returned.

Death was a part of life. It was a part of life that I could not change no matter how fearful or anxious I was by the loss of my father. I had to accept that I had lost the only person I could talk to outside of therapy. I had to accept the loss of my best friend. So, I had to find a new best friend. I was going to discover my new best friend with the help of my passion for writing. I was going to find that I was going to be my new best friend once I lost my father. I spent hour after hour writing about the loss of my father. This time that I spent writing was helping me reconnect with my old best friend, my father, and find that I was my new best friend.

I eventually found that I was not feeling so depressed about the loss of my father anymore. I was not feeling so depressed by his loss anymore because my memories of him were inspiring me to move forward. So, I was ready to get back to my spiritual journey without him. Sadly, I could not do anything about losing someone I felt so comfortable around socially. So, the death of my father was still a devastating loss for my battle with social anxiety. I knew that every time I left my world of isolation, I was going to feel the loss of my father. I knew I was going to feel my father's loss since I was still someone who was unable to socialize with people.

The loss of my father took away the one person I was socially comfortable around. So, the death of my father was a major loss for me socially. However, my passion for writing helped me to heal from this loss. My passion for writing helped me to deal with the death of my father with its ability to allow me to have a safe place to feel comfortable enough to share my thoughts. These thoughts were mostly about my fear and anxiety about not being able to speak to my father anymore and about how I might be more socially isolated. I was finding that this safe place to express myself was a powerful tool for me to deal with loss. As I found strength from my passion for writing with its power to heal, I was ready to move forward. I was ready to confront reality. I found I was ready to find a way to start living my life without my best friend.

Life Without My Best Friend

I had to find a way to live life without my best friend after the death of my father. I started to learn how to live my life without him by first trying to return to my old daily routine. It took me about a day or two before I was ready to even try to return to my old daily routine though, because I was feeling so guilty about leaving my mother home alone after his death. I was not sure how my mother was doing after my father's death because we did not talk much. We did not talk much after his death because we both suffered from social anxiety. At least, it was my belief that my mother also suffered from social anxiety. I will never know this for certain or not though since this is not something, we ever have been able to discuss. My mother and I have never had deep conversations about anything important or meaningful. This is mostly due to our fear of confrontation. Again, this is what I believe. I do not know, and I may never know if this is true or not since we are unable to talk to each other about such things. I hope someday this might all change since I have always wanted a closer connection with my mother.

I never had much of a problem talking to my father because he was always socially assertive. My father was always able to talk about something. Most of the things that he liked to talk about with me led to arguments because I think he thrived upon confrontation. I was not to fond of arguing with him because I hated leaving angry after talking to him. However, I liked that I could always talk to him. Then, those rare moments when I did feel socially uncomfortable around him, I could simply leave because I always knew where to find him again. I knew my father was always going to be at his spot within the garage unless he went to bed. Sadly, I never did feel this same social comfort with my mother because of us both having social anxiety. So, the death of my father not only meant the loss of my best friend, it also meant the loss of the only person that I was socially comfortable around. I was hoping to change all of this though, after my father passed away. I was hoping to build a closer relationship with my beloved mother after my father's death. A relationship where we could talk to each other more.

My mother and I never felt socially comfortable around each other. My mother was always caring and financially supportive. I always knew that my mother was the one to call if I needed help with something. My father rarely helped me with anything. Maybe, this was his way of trying to be a good parent since he was trying to teach me about responsibility. I always resented him for this though, and it led us to having many heated arguments. Eventually, I stopped asking him for help because of these arguments. Instead, I turned to my mother for help when I needed it. My mother rarely said no when I asked for help. She may have gotten upset about me always asking for help. However, she rarely said no. I loved my mom for always bailing me out because I felt I never had to suffer when she was around. Yet, I could see how this might not have been helping me either. I could see how bailing me out was keeping me from learning about responsibility. So, I saw how both my parents were teaching me something.

My mother was always the responsible parent. I do not know where me or my father might be today if it were not for my mother being so responsible. Unfortunately, as important as my mother was to my survival, I never had a great social connection with her. So, as I left the house to start to return to my old daily routines, I was worried about leaving her alone. This was making me anxious about returning to my old daily routines at the library. At home we both found our way back to our old daily routines. I was back to my passion for writing. My mother was back to doing puzzles and watching television. However, neither one of us were ready to return to the real world and deal with the rest of humanity. I needed about two days before I was ready to return to the real world. My mother needed more time at home because she had the more difficult task of returning to work when she returned to the real world. I was only returning to my world of isolation at the library to pursue my passion for writing. So, I did not have to interact with people. The only time I had to interact with people was when I was at Portage Path.

I found it more difficult to deal with the death of my father when I was at Portage Path. These days were more difficult since I had to socialize with people. I did not mind seeing my therapist; however, I could not deal with going to my support groups. Anytime, I needed to socialize with more than one person my social anxiety returned, and I felt the loss of my father.

I had been coping rather well with the death of my father. My passion for writing was the reason why I was coping so well with the death of my father. This was why I felt like it was so important to get back to my old daily routine. I knew that I had to get back to the library because this was where I found my inspiration for my passion for writing. I had to get back to my beautiful blonde library angel and the other library angels. Once I got to the library, I was going to learn that my old daily routine had changed because I did not have my father anymore. The loss of my father meant that I did not have anyone to talk to before I went to the library and when I got home anymore. Many of these discussions were about my passion for writing and the beautiful blonde library angel and her friends. The loss of these conversations with my father made it difficult to leave and to return home. This was only a minor change to my old daily routine. However, it had a great impact upon my social anxiety and how I dealt with humanity.

The impact the loss of my father had upon my social anxiety and my return to the real world could never be stated strongly enough. My father was truly my best friend because he was the only person who I was able to be socially comfortable around. I had very few people during my life that I felt socially comfortable around. There was my best friend from Florida. There was my French grandmother. There was Pierre-Yves. Finally, there were my therapists. However, all of these individuals were only a part of my life temporarily. My father was the one constant. He was the one person that was always there for me to feel socially comfortable around until he passed away. So, the loss of my father was devastating to my social existence.

The death of my father meant that I was going to have to find some way of communicating with the rest of the world without having to socialize. The only place that was left for me to feel socially comfortable was when I went to talk to my therapist. Unfortunately, I had a therapist that was not working for me when my father passed away. I was trying to build a relationship with this therapist because he had a good reputation for being a good therapist. However, the chemistry was not working between us. Hence, I felt as if I had nobody to go to for social support when my father passed away. This lack of social support made it difficult for me to want to leave the house. I could not cope with the feelings of being left all alone with nobody for social support. The only place I was able to find some comfort was with my writing.

I felt everyone was judging me because of my social anxiety. My father was the only person I did not feel was judging me because he was always too busy judging himself. So, I felt as if there was always someone worse off than I was when my father was alive. I guess the saying of misery loves company is true because this was how I felt when my father was alive. Sadly, now, my father was gone, and I had to learn how to live within a world without him. I felt I was all alone after his passing. I was not sure how I was going to move forward feeling so socially isolated. So, I turned to the only source of strength I had left. I turned to my passion for writing. The instant I entered my world of isolation at the library and turned to my passion for writing my social anxiety disappeared. Then, as soon as I left this world of isolation it returned. So, I was spending every day at the library with my passion for writing after his death.

I was writing about the memories I had of my father because they helped me to stay spiritually connected to him. I wrote about our great road trip we took together visiting French Castles. I wrote about My Wonderful French Childhood. I wrote about all the wonderful conversations we had while he was still alive. Lastly, I wrote about his love for Celtic Music.

My father loved Celtic music. He loved his Celtic music as much as I loved my French music. He may have even loved it more since it was all he listened to most of the time. His love for Celtic music was probably my greatest memory of him. So, as I spent my time writing about my father, I also listened to Celtic music since it strengthened my spiritual connection to him. Pavarotti's music also helped strengthen my spiritual connection to him because as a child I thought this was his favorite singer. I later found out that I was wrong about this, yet I always believed this to be true. I even bought him a video of one of Pavarotti's concerts and I started watching this video every Christmas Eve until I had no way of watching it anymore. This was going to turn into a Christmas Eve tradition for me for most of my life. I still continue this tradition today. The only change to this tradition was that I now watched the concert with my computer. This was my introduction to Pavarotti and his voice. I believe his voice is one of the most beautiful voices I have ever heard. What makes this music that much more powerful though is the powerful spiritual connection that I feel to my father whenever I listen to Pavarotti.

My connection with my father was never more powerful than when I was listening to Celtic music and Pavarotti. What made this connection even more powerful was that when I was listening to it after his death, I was also pursuing my passion for writing. My passion for writing was my way of healing from the devastating loss of my father. Once I was done writing my seventy pages about my father after his death, I was ready to move forward. I was ready to integrate the lifestyle changes I had planned to be a more passionate writer before his death. However, before integrating these lifestyle changes, I felt the need to try to push myself to confront my social anxiety again because I was worried, I might not leave my world of isolation.

I tried to push myself to confront my social anxiety by going to a support group at Portage Path. I walked downstairs to the garage knowing that my father was not going to be at his usual spot anymore. I was still able to feel his presence though as I went to get my shoes before leaving the house to go to therapy. I thought about what he might say to me and then I thought about how I might respond. Usually, we simply said hello and goodbye and then he asked me about my plans for the day. My usual response was that I was going to see the beautiful blonde library angel and her friends. Although, this was not all that we liked to discuss.

My father loved to tease me about Lebron James if he was playing since he knew how much I really disliked Lebron as a basketball player. I did not dislike him so much as a person per say because I had a great deal of respect for him as a person. I was always able to separate the man from his work and I always had a great deal of respect for Lebron as a man. However, I hated him as a player because I was such a Steph Currie and Michael Jordan fan. I could not stand it when people talked about him being compared to Michael Jordan. These were only some of the things that we liked to discuss when I was leaving the house and as I returned home.

Some other topics we liked to discuss were politics and soaps. My father's soaps of choice were Young and the Restless and Bold and the Beautiful. My favorite soap to watch was Guiding Light until it was cancelled. Then, I continued to watch soaps after it was cancelled, although my reason for watching soaps changed. I was watching soaps for the beautiful women.

I was finally able to leave the house and start my trip toward Portage Path. This was going to be a dark trip to Portage Path. It was going to be a dark trip because of all my negative thoughts I was having during my trip there. These dark, negative thoughts were not about the death of my father though, instead they were about my need to return to work. It was not surprising that these were my dark thoughts after his death since I always felt like work was hell.

These were the negative thoughts I was having before I finally got to Portage Path. I could not stand being around so many people once I got to Portage Path. So, I had to go outside and wait for group to start. I only had to wait about fifteen minutes for group to start, yet I felt like these fifteen minutes were taking forever. Finally, this support group started, and I was able to stay there the entire group. I was able to stay the entire group despite the heat and my social anxiety. This was mostly due to my invisible man complex being triggered, so I could not leave.

I wanted nothing more than to go home and talk to my father after I finally left this support group. I wanted to tell him about the dark thoughts I was having about having to return to work again. Sadly, I knew that this was not possible, so I knew I was going to have to find another outlet for these dark thoughts I was having. I knew I had to turn to my passion for writing once more. My passion for writing was gradually helping me heal from the devastating loss of my father. I believed my passion for writing was going to help me find strength from the death of my father because of how it helped me get over so many other losses already. My passion for writing had already helped me find my way out of my pit of darkness. It also helped me to deal with the loss of my car and my work at the group home. I was starting to view losses differently now. I saw losses as challenges to learn from and as opportunities to grow rather than as paths to my pit of darkness. The loss of my father was devastating; however, it was not going to be the last major loss of my life. I knew that someday I was going to also have deal with losing my mother. Then, I was going to be all alone unless I was able to find a way to socialize.

I started thinking about my death a great deal after the death of my father as well. I mostly thought about my greatest fear though which was never attaining a beautiful woman. I knew there was only one way to change this possible future, and this was to build my confidence. I knew of only one way to build my confidence, and this was through my writing.

Writing was my life. I was never going to stop writing. However, I also knew I was going to need to find a way to balance all this writing with my other needs. Before, my father's death I had made plans to start writing ten pages a day. These were still my plans after my father's death. So, after I grieved over the loss of my father, I was writing about ten pages a day.

I found I had to really focus to write ten pages a day. I found that when I could really focus, I could write ten pages a day within about five hours. I found that writing the pages of my book was much less time consuming than rewriting my book. I found it took a great deal more time to rewrite and edit the pages I wrote of my book because when I was rewriting and editing, I was trying to make each sentence perfect. Thus, rewriting my book was much more difficult and time consuming. Each time that I went over these sentences, I felt I could do better and make them more perfect. So, I learned a valuable lesson while rewriting. I learned that being a great writer was more about a gut feeling then it was about perfection. This gut feeling was going to be a valuable lesson to learn because the more I felt this gut feeling, the more confident that I got. This confidence was then helping me to find the strength to return to reality.

I spent more and more time rewriting the pages of my book. This time that I spent rewriting was helping me gain more and more confidence. I found it was difficult to plan for this rewriting time though because there were times when I could rewrite a page within an hour. Then, there were other times when it took me several hours to feel that gut feeling from writing a page. I never minded the time it took though because I always loved the joy of the journey. I never felt there was enough time for me to get to all the rewriting I wanted to accomplish. I always felt rushed to complete these pages. This leads me to the main reason why I hated work. I hated to work because every hour that I was spending at work was an hour away from my passion for writing. This was why I was finding it more and more difficult to keep regular work.

I had to work and make money to help my mom with the bills. I had to work because I knew I needed money to get my book published. However, I was not ready to return to work yet. I knew I needed more time to build my confidence with my passion for writing before I was ready to return to work. So, I started spending everyday at the library pursuing my passion for writing after my father's death. I loved my time at the library because I loved being isolated and alone. I loved spending this time with my new best friend, myself. My time alone has always been the best time of my life since I knew what I liked and what made me comfortable. I knew how much I loved the cold and certain types of music. I knew I did not have to please anyone else if I was alone. So, this was how I wanted to live my life. The only time when I did not enjoy being isolated and alone were those moments when I wanted to be with a beautiful woman.

I wanted nothing more than to share my life with a beautiful woman. I wanted nothing more than to find a beautiful woman that I could feel socially comfortable around. I did not want to live the rest of my life all alone obsessing over beautiful women. I still held out hope that I might one day find the woman of my dreams. However, I was not willing to let go of my passion for writing to be with her since I believed my passion for writing was equally important.

The death of my father was a devastating loss. I lost the only person I was socially comfortable around outside of therapy. My passion for writing helped me live my life without my best friend by helping me to heal from his loss. Once it helped me to heal, I was ready to move forward. Yet, moving forward did not mean I was ready to forget my father. I could never forget my father and I will never have to because I will always feel his spirit within my writings. One thing I always admired about my father was that he always knew his passions. My father always had a passion for cooking, gardening, watching TV, and he loved the heat. He even found a way to get paid for one of his passions. My father spent his entire life as a French chef.

It was my belief that everyone had a passion. My passion was my passion for writing. My mother's passion was her passion for sewing. My grandmother's passion was for gardening. Finally, my father's passion was for cooking. My father also had a passion for gardening and farming. However, cooking was his true passion, and he was really great at it because they offered him his own TV Show as a French chef. However, he turned it down because he was afraid of cooking with all those people watching. So, my father knew something about social anxiety. My father was lucky enough though to turn his passion into a career. When I look back upon my father's life, I realize that he had an incredible life. He was able to make money with one of his passions. He was able to move to another country and succeed for the most part since he met and married the woman of his dreams and had a family with her. Finally, he also had the courage to successfully move several times. Sadly, I could never tell my father how much I admired him because I was not aware of all of this until I wrote about him after he passed away.

This is a regret that I will have to learn to live with for the rest of my life. I have to accept the fact that I will never be able to verbally tell him how much I admired him. The only way that I will be able to express my admiration for him is with my passion for writing. My ability to express my admiration for him with my passion for writing was helping me to heal. So, my passion for writing was once again showing me its power to heal by helping me to get over another loss. After I was done with expressing my admiration for my father, I was starting to feel inspired to deal with work again. I knew it was going to be difficult to return to a world without my best friend. I knew it was going to be difficult to not have him to socialize with every day. However, I also knew that I had my passion for writing to turn to after the loss of my father. So, I was spending hours upon hours with my passion for writing after his death. Eventually, I started to be my new best friend and I was ready to live life without my best friend.

Moving Forward

It was time for me to start moving forward with the rest of my life. I spent a week at home grieving over the death of my father with my passion for writing. Before that, I spent the previous week grieving over the pain and disappointment of being rejected by Annabelle 2. Thus, a good two weeks had now passed since I last went to the library to feel its magic. This meant that a good two weeks had also passed since I last saw my beautiful blonde library angel. I never spent so much time away from her before. Before my break from the library, I maybe went a few days without seeing her because of work. However, even during those few days I still went to get a glimpse of her beauty before and after I went to work. So, I was ready to return to the library to see my beautiful blonde library angel, even if it meant seeing Annabelle 2.

The last time that I was going to see Annabelle 2 at the library was when I saw her running into the library to checkout a stack of books. I was going to see her returning her books a few days after I saw her working at the library for the last time. I always thought that once these library angels quit working at the library, I was never going to see them again. I thought once they quit, they were going to be going off to college and disappear from my life forever. Then, I saw her eating lunch at the French Bistro a few days later and I realized my spiritual journey with them was not over. I did not expect to see Annabelle 2 there that day. I was simply going there do some writing since the library was closed. Then, once I got there, I decided to sit by the fireplace because this was where I got the best view of the beautiful angels working there. I started to do some writing and as I took a break from my writing, I saw her sitting there. Once I saw her, I could not focus upon my writing anymore. I was too distracted by her beauty and what her presence meant to my spiritual journey. I knew her reappearance had to mean something. I was not that sure what it meant; however, I was sure that it had to mean something.

I was not sure why Annabelle reappeared into my life that day at the French Bistro. I already knew that she rejected my letter after I tried to give it to her. Thus, her reappearance was not about her being interested. So, what did her reappearance mean for my spiritual journey. I was trying to figure this out as I saw her having lunch with her family. Then, I saw that she was also sitting with her boyfriend and maybe his family as well. At first, when I saw her with her boyfriend it was very painful. Then, I thought back to when she was at the library and I remembered her wearing an engagement ring. I blocked out the engagement ring at the library because I wanted to believe I had a chance with her so much. Sadly, this time I found it impossible to block it out, and once I saw it, I was happy to see it since it gave me some closure.

I was grateful to Annabelle 2 for reappearing into my life. I was grateful to her for her reappearance because it gave me some closure to why she had rejected my letter. Closure was an important step toward me finding a way to move forward. I already had this mental closure with her with my passion for writing after she rejected my letter. Then, I saw her wearing the engagement ring again and I believed I was getting my real closure with her at the French Bistro.

I learned that my passion for writing was going to be the best way to work through all future pain and loss I was ever going to have within my life. My passion for writing was going to help me find strength from this pain and loss. However, this does not mean that I always thought the benefit was worth the pain. There was nothing I could do about the losses and rejections I had to endure though, and I knew pain and loss were a part of life. However, I also believed it was important to learn lessons from pain and loss. I thought these lessons were important to life. I believed the lesson I learned from being rejected by Annabelle 2 and the death of my father was how my passion for writing had the power to heal. My passion for writing helped me find a way through all of this devastating loss by giving me a reason to live.

My passion for writing was my reason for living. I knew if I was ever going to move forward then it was going to be with the help of my passion for writing. I knew I was not going to let anything be more of a priority to me than my passion for writing. Thus, as I was ready to move forward with my life, there was only one acceptable way for me to start the process. I was going to start the process of moving forward by a return to the library and my obsessions. I knew that I had to return to my world of isolation at the library to write my book. It was November 2017 when I was ready to return to writing my first book about my spiritual journey.

I was so excited to return to the writing of my first book after suffering these two devastating losses of my father and Annabelle 2. I was so excited because I wanted to see where the strength of my passion for writing was going to take me after discovering its power to heal. The pain and disappointment of being rejected by Annabelle 2 and the death of my father were still present. However, my passion for writing had given me a different view of these two devastating losses. I found that out of the despair that I felt from these two losses I could discover strength from them as well. I was able to find this strength with my passion for writing.

The strength I found from my passion for writing had me very excited about moving forward. I knew the first step to moving forward was going to be with me writing my first book. I started my return to writing my first book by first looking at my plans for how I was going to devote more time to writing it. I was looking to see how I was going to find more time to write more pages every day. I was going to need the time to go from writing two pages a day to writing ten pages a day. I was going to be writing ten pages a day nonstop either at the library or at home until I completed my book. My focus during the month of September was about trying to write my first book as soon as possible. I still had fourteen twenty-page chapters left to complete before I completed my book. I was focused upon nothing else other than completing it.

It took me about a month and a half to complete my first book. I was focusing all my energy toward completing my first book. I spent every minute and every hour writing to finally reach my goal of completing my first book. As I wrote my first book, I started to visualize my path toward being a published writer. I thought if I continued writing at this pace, I could get my book completed by the middle of December. Then, I started thinking about my future plans for writing. I was thinking that if I kept writing at this pace all my life, I could have two books completed every year. I was thinking that the more books I wrote the better my chances were of someday getting published, so I kept writing. I also found that my creativity was constantly improving the more that I kept writing. Thus, out of my loss I found my writing was at its peak.

I was living some of the best moments of my life while at the peak of my writing. I returned to my world of isolation at the library. I also returned to my beautiful blonde library angel and the other library angels who were still at the library. However, as I returned to the library, I was going to find that the library angels were disappearing. The number of library angels at the library already started to dwindle at the start of my spiritual journey. The numbers started to dwindle with the loss of the one angel who was only there for a short time. The first angel that disappeared was not a major loss. She was not a major loss because she was only there for about a month. Also, my passion for writing had not developed yet, hence I never really did create an image of her as an angel. Thus, there were only four angels when I returned.

The first of these four angels that I was going to lose after returning to the library was going to be the beautiful Irish library angel. This was the only library angel that worked during the day at the library. All the other library angels were working from four to eight the weekdays or four hours every Saturday, nine to one or one to five. This was why this library angel was more special than the rest. Sadly, I was starting to notice that she was not at the library anymore after my break from the library. I remember looking for her and not finding her anywhere. It took about two weeks for me to realize that she was gone for good. This was going to be a major loss for two reasons. One reason why it was such a loss was because she was so beautiful and friendly. The other reason was because I was losing another connection to my father. I was losing this connection to him because he was the one who identified her as being an Irish angel.

My passion for writing helped me to heal from the loss of another connection to my father. I always knew that these library angels were only going to be a part of my life for a short time because most of them were only students. I thought the Irish angel might remain at the library though because she was a library employee, not a student assistant. I was sadly mistaken.

There were three library angels left after the loss of the beautiful Irish library angel. Annabelle 2 was still working at the library once I returned from my break from the library. The beautiful creative brunette library angel was still at the library. Finally, there was the beautiful blonde library angel who was still there. Yes, my beautiful blonde library angel was still present.

My beautiful blonde library angel was the one constant at the library. She was why I started going to the library at the start of my spiritual journey. She was why I continued going to the library as the other library angels were starting to disappear. I knew I was never going to stop going to the library if she was still at the library. I knew that I was not going anywhere if she was still at the library because she was the spark that started my spiritual journey. I knew I never could attain her because of her being so young and attractive. However, my spiritual journey with her was never about attaining her. My spiritual journey with her was always about the spiritual energy she brought to my passion for writing. This spiritual energy was giving me hope and building my confidence through my passion for writing. Thus, I was not going anywhere if she was still at the library because she was the beautiful angel that led to my rebirth.

My spiritual journey with her was going to continue for the rest of my life. I could not imagine there ever being a time when she was not a part of my life. I knew that it was still going to continue once she physically left the library. I knew it was even going to continue after I left the library because I still feel her spiritual energy within my passion for writing today. However, she had not left the library when I returned from my break. She was still one of my library angels when I returned from my break and she remained present until I completed my first book.

The first book that I published was called *The Beautiful Blonde Library Angel*. I was calling it this since it was about the angel who was the one constant during my spiritual journey. She did finally leave my side after I published my first book. However, my beautiful blonde library angel was the one constant at the library until I finally wrote and published my first book.

I found my spiritual inspiration from the unlikeliest of places. I was not looking for spiritual inspiration. However, once my spiritual inspiration appeared, I was unwilling to let it go since it was so powerful. So, when I was ready to return from these two major losses I returned to my source of inspiration. I returned to the library and my passion for writing. Once I got back to my passion for writing I spent the following two months devoted to it. I was writing ten pages a day seven days a week from September 2017 to October of 2017. Sadly, I could not spend all my time at the library writing without thinking about returning to work. I knew I was going to have to find work again. However, after these two devastating losses I was not ready to deal with humanity or work again. So, it took me a few weeks before I was ready to look for work again. Luckily, I found work quickly once I finally started looking. I only had to apply to about five places before I was offered work at two places. When I was offered work, I had the opportunity to work at either a grocery store or a call center. I had a difficult time choosing between the two since I was trying to make the best choice for my writing. I knew I had to start to work. However, I did not want to sacrifice too much of my writing time for work. The running theme of my life was always that I valued my time more than I valued needing money.

I had to decide between the call center and the grocery store. The call center meant working farther away than the grocery store. However, it also meant making more money since I got more hours there. It took me awhile to make a decision since I was thinking about others more than myself. I knew working at the grocery store was the right decision for me since it gave me more time to write. So, the idea of making more money was appealing because I so wanted a car. However, I was unwilling to sacrifice my writing time to make this money. Hence, I chose my passion for writing over needing money. I chose to work at the grocery store.

Adding work to my new daily routine involved me having to try to find a way to find balance. I was going to have to find a way to be able to balance my time between going to work and my passion for writing. My first day of training at this grocery store was November 20th, 2017. My first day of training only lasted for about three hours and it was a very boring Monday of watching videos. I was already thinking about the negative aspects about working at this grocery store. I was already thinking about how I was not going to get many hours by working here. Also, I was only getting minimum wage. So, my attitude about working at this grocery store already went from excitement to disappointment. However, the one good thing about my first day of work there was that my mom let me drive her car. So, I was able to drive home and listen to some music to escape the misery of my first day of work. My mother letting me drive her car was great toward me moving forward since it reminded me of how much I wanted a car. This reminder of me wanting a car led me to start thinking about my plans of getting one. I was going to start saving for a car my first day of training at this grocery store. I spent most of training thinking about how much I needed for a car if I remained at this grocery store. I was thinking it was going to take me about ten years to get a car which was disheartening. So, I knew I was going to need more than my work at this grocery store if I ever wanted to get a car.

My passion for writing was my reason for choosing this work at a grocery store. I was simply unwilling to sacrifice my passion for writing for my need to make money. I was thinking that working less hours was my way to balance my need for money with my passion for writing. At first, I was feeling comfortable with this decision. However, I knew that eventually I was going to have to look for some other employment if I had any hope of ever getting myself a car.

My wanting a car was a great motivator for me to move forward. I had my passion for writing, and this was a great way to spend my time when I was not working. However, I needed to work to make money. The problem was that I did not have a reason to make money and this made it difficult for me to find and keep work. However, when I was reminded of my wanting a car this all changed. My wanting a car was going to lead me to finding the right balance for working and to continue to pursue my passion for writing. I had returned to my path of moving forward with my work at this grocery store. I was finding the time to work and to write. Then, I got an email from Bon Gout and they were offering me another opportunity to work for them. This was great because I was still holding out hope that I might be able to return to work for them someday. However, when the stopped contacting me, I feared all hope of returning to work for them might be gone. Then, five months went by and I finally heard from them via email. I was thrilled to get the opportunity to return to Bon Gout once I heard from them. Then, things got even better because the grocery store was willing to keep me when I was off from Bon Gout. So, now, I was going to be able to start saving for a car because I was going to be making some good money since I was going to be working seven days a week. This meant that now the challenge was going to be more about me finding a way to continue with my passion for writing.

The following few months I was able find a way to balance my time between my employment at Bon Gout and my passion for writing. I was working at Bon Gout Wednesday to Sunday from ten to five. Then, I was working at the grocery store Monday and Tuesday from seven to two. I was working seven days a week which was great for me financially and it was going to help me to eventually get a car. It was going to take me about five months to save enough money to get a car. I was worried that working so much might lead me to losing my passion for writing, however this never did happen. I found a way to continue writing as I worked all of these hours because my locations of inspiration were right near where I worked.

I spent my days going to work and then after work I went to the library to see the beautiful library angels. This was my new daily routine for about five months unless I took a day off, I rarely took a day off though because I wanted a car. During this time that I spent working and writing, I was finding that it was getting quite difficult for me to get to my writing.

I never lost my passion for writing while working so much. I was not going to let go of my passion for writing because it was my reason for living. So, I wrote when I was not working. The more time I wrote, the more I started to question whether I wanted to have my first book be about my life anymore. However, I never stopped writing. I never took a break from my writing because I feared what this might mean for my future as a writer. So, I continued writing despite my doubts and fears. My doubts and fears were more about not having enough time, then they were about a lack of passion for writing. I never questioned my passion. My passion was never stronger than it was after my two devastating losses. Yet, I could see others taking me from my passion because I felt they might not understand me spending so much time alone and isolated. So, I feared taking this break because I thought the rest of the world might keep me from returning to my passion for writing if I took this break. Hence, I started spending all of my time isolated and alone trying to make it as a writer. I still continued to work and make money whenever possible though because I knew I needed money to publish my book and to get a car.

I was starting to find a balance. I was working to make the money I needed to get my book published and to get a car. I was spending the rest of my time with my passion for writing. My passion for writing was giving me the confidence to deal with humanity again. So, I was never going to stop cultivating my passion for writing. I found the strength to confront my debilitating social anxiety by turning to my passion for writing to gain the strength to confront it.

I found it especially difficult to deal with my social anxiety during Thanksgiving. Thanksgiving was such a difficult time for me because I had to go to one of our family dinners. I was going to have to suffer through one of these family dinners Saturday November 25th, 2017. This was the first family dinner since my father passed away. So, I felt I had to go to it for my father and to practice socializing with people more. The worst part of this Thanksgiving dinner was when I had to get the Turkey meat. I was trying to get it as quickly as possible because I hated being the center of attention while trying to get it. Then, the turkey meat started falling off the fork and the more I tried to get it the more it kept falling off the fork. I must have tried about five times before I finally got the turkey meat. I finally got back to my seat after this and realized I had to go to my mom's car for my Polar Pop. So, I had to suffer, through my social anxiety once more to get it. Finally, I got back to my seat with my Polar Pop and I remained there the rest of the night. The rest of the night was going to be very boring and uncomfortable.

This Thanksgiving dinner was an especially uncomfortable Thanksgiving dinner since this was when everyone wanted to say goodbye to my father. This was a mere formality for me though since I already grieved over his death with my passion for writing. After this uncomfortable Thanksgiving dinner, I started moving forward with a new location of inspiration.

My New Location
Of Inspiration

My new location of inspiration was this French Bistro that was near my work at Bon Gout. The library near my house was my original location of inspiration. I was spending most of my time at the library as I started my spiritual journey. There were two reasons why I was spending most of my time there. The first reason why I was spending most of my time there was that this was where my beautiful blonde library angel was working. My beautiful blonde library angel introduced me to the magic of the library. Then, I discovered four other beautiful angels working there and its magic only intensified. These beautiful library angels were the main reason why the library near my house was going to turn into my original location of inspiration.

Another reason why the library was going to be my original location of inspiration was because of its location. The library was only a short distance from my house. It only took about five or ten minutes to get there by car based upon the speed you went and all the traffic. Then, I discovered that it only took about a half an hour to walk there after the loss of my car. These walks to and from the library had the added benefit of getting me to start exercising every day. The loss of my car was not something I was happy about because I hated losing the freedom of being able to do what I wanted when I wanted. However, when I think about the loss of my car today, I believe that this loss might have been a good thing. I see the loss of my car as possibly having been a good thing today because it got me to start exercising. The key to me starting to exercise though was that I was not thinking about exercising. When I started exercising, I was not thinking about my need to be healthier or my need to lose weight. My motivation for walking to the library every day was about me wanting to see my beautiful blonde library angel.

I was unwilling to let go of the spiritual energy I felt from seeing my beautiful blonde library angel at the library every day. I was not willing to let anything stand between me and the power of my beautiful blonde library angel. So, after I got over the grief of losing my car, I started walking to the library every day to see her. This was now a part of my spiritual journey with her.

I continued walking to and from the library throughout the first year of my spiritual journey with my beautiful blonde library angel. This path of walking to and from the library was working out great for me when I was out of work. This path was even working out great for me when I was only working at the grocery store. However, the times when these walks stopped working out that great for me were those times when I started my employment at Bon Gout. These walks to the library stopped working out great for me because my mom was starting to let me borrow her car when I started to work at both the grocery store and at Bon Gout as well. Once, I started borrowing my mom's car I remembered what I was missing, and I did not want to waste my time walking to and from the library anymore. So, I still felt the magic of the library when the beautiful blonde library angel was working. However, it was the times when my beautiful blonde library angel stopped working at the library that the library was losing its magic.

My mom letting me borrow the car was leading us into several very heated arguments with each other. These arguments were the part of reality that was making it so difficult for me to stay at the library when the beautiful blonde library angel was not working. It was still working when she was working because she was all that mattered when she was working. The rest of the time these heated arguments with my mother were affecting my time at the library. What also did not help was that during the times when she was not working, none of the other library angels were working there to inspire my writing either. Annabelle 2 stopped working at the library, so the only other library angel who was left was the beautiful creative library angel. Then, what made things even worse, was that my two library angels were usually working together. Monday, Wednesday, and Saturday mornings these two beautiful library angels were working together. Then, Tuesdays it was only my creative angel. Finally, Wednesdays my beautiful blonde library angel was working by herself. The rest of the time there were no angels.

My mother started letting me borrow her car when I started working at both Bon Gout and the grocery store after the death of my father. I was very excited to have this opportunity to drive again because it reminded me of my passion for driving. This passion I had for driving was initially what led me to pursuing a career as a truck driver. Initially, when my mom let me borrow her car I was going back and forth between the library and work. However, these drives between Bon Gout and the library were leading us into having many arguments. My mother did not like that I was driving around so much because she was leasing her car. She did not appreciate me putting so many miles upon her car every time I got the car. However, I was unwilling to let go of my obsession with the beautiful blonde library angel. These opposing views were going to lead us to having arguments every day. These arguments were difficult to ignore when I was at the library without my library angels. One reason why I was having trouble ignoring these arguments was that I could understand her side of the argument. I could understand how she was doing me a favor by letting me borrow her car. I could understand how letting me borrow her car was a special privilege because this car was also a brand-new car. I did not like feeling like I was taking advantage of this special privilege. So, I was starting to feel a great deal of anxiety when I was at the library and none of my library angels were present. Unfortunately, this anxiety when they were not present was making me not enjoy my time there.

The main reason why I had such a difficult time enjoying my time at the library was because I did not like arguing with my mother so much after the death of my father. My mom was the only real relationship I had left after the death of my father. I also had all of my therapists, yet they were only by appointments. Then, the rest of the time all I had was my mom.

These arguments I had with my mother were keeping me from enjoying my time at the library when the library angels were not present. The anxiety I was feeling from these arguments was even making it difficult for me to enjoy my time at the library when they were present. So, this was when I knew I had to find a way to put a stop to the arguments. I was still not willing to lose the power of the beautiful blonde library angel. I knew I still wanted to go to the library when she was working. I also wanted to try and be there those days when the beautiful creative library angel was working, then the rest of the time I did not care about being there that much. Hence, I knew I was ready to start looking for another location of inspiration, and my search introduced me to this French Bistro that was located right across the intersection from Bon Gout.

This French Bistro turned into my new location of inspiration when I was going to discover my first beautiful angel outside the library there one day. This beautiful angel from the French Bistro was one of the most beautiful angels I ever saw. The beautiful blonde library angel will always be the most powerful of all my angels. She will always be the most powerful because she was the one who gave birth to my spiritual journey. My beautiful blonde library angel appeared into my life at a time when I lost all hope of a better future. The beauty and timing of my beautiful blonde librarian was why she was so powerful. Yet, as powerful as she was, there were times I questioned whether she was the most beautiful women I ever saw. However, the one thing that I never questioned was the spiritual energy she had over my journey.

My beautiful blonde library angel was definitely beautiful because she had the most angelic face I had ever seen. She literally had the face of an angel. This was the original reason why I started calling her my beautiful blonde library angel. However, as beautiful as she truly was, this was not what made her so special. The reason why she was so special was more because of the timing of when she entered my life. She arrived into my life at a time when I lost all hope of ever having a better future. So, her angelic face and timing were what made this beautiful blonde library angel so powerful. Another reason why she was so powerful was that she helped me to make a very powerful decision. This powerful decision was going to be to follow my obsession with her wherever it might lead. Finally, her consistency made her special.

The loss of my beautiful blonde library angel was something I could not imagine since she was the one constant while writing my first book. She was always able to inspire my passion for writing. She gave birth to my passion for writing. She inspired me and guided me out of my pit of darkness. She inspired my return to the library after my two devastating losses. She also continues to inspire my passion for writing with her spiritual energy today. My beautiful blonde library angel has not physically been a part of my spiritual journey for about a year now. Yet, her spiritual energy still continues to be a part of my spiritual journey through my passion for writing. Also, I continue to feel her presence with my many obsessions with the beautiful angels at the French Bistro. I was not sure how I was going to continue my life as a writer once I lost my beautiful blonde library angel. However, today, I know that I am able to live without her physical presence because I am still able to feel her spiritual energy with my passion for writing.

I took my first step toward learning how to live without the physical presence of my beautiful blonde library angel at the French Bistro. I took my first step as I got my first glimpse of this beautiful angel with black hair and glasses as I walked into the French Bistro. The first thing that I noticed about this beautiful black haired angel was her amazing body. I could tell when I saw her body that she was out of my league. There was no way someone who looked that beautiful could ever be attracted to someone who had so many inadequacies. Yet, I did not care because I wanted to continue to see her beauty even if I had no chance with her. Thus, started my spiritual journey without the physical presence of my beautiful blonde library angel.

The beautiful angel from the French Bistro was helping me learn to live without the physical presence of the beautiful blonde library angel. This was going to be an important thing to realize when my beautiful blonde library angel actually left. It was a valuable lesson to learn because it helped me to see that there were other beautiful angels outside the library. As I continued my spiritual journey, I started to discover there was a great variety of beautiful angels.

The beautiful black haired angel from the French Bistro was only going to be a part of my spiritual journey for a short time. She was only going to be a part of my spiritual journey for about two months. I first discovered my black haired angel at the French Bistro at the start of 2018. It was probably sometime around March that I first saw her there and then she left at the start of the summer of 2018. So, I did not have much time with this beautiful black haired at the French Bistro. However, even though I did not have much time with her, and I may not have a clear memory of what this angel looked like today, I do still feel her spiritual presence. I continue to feel her spiritual presence as I write about my spiritual journey with all my angels.

This beautiful angel from the French Bistro was the first beautiful angel to teach me about transference. She introduced me to this concept by showing me that I could feel the same spiritual energy I felt from the beautiful blonde library angel with other beautiful angels. This was something I started to realize with the other beautiful library angels. Although, I was not fully aware of this concept until I felt it with my first beautiful angel outside of the library. Hence, it took discovering a new angel at a new location of inspiration to learn of this concept.

There was more to this angel from the French Bistro than mere beauty. I was also to discover that this beautiful black haired angel was also very friendly. I was going to first learn about how friendly she was when she smiled at me and said hello to me when I first arrived. This beautiful black haired angel even went beyond saying a simple hello and she started asking me about my day. This was probably her simply having an outgoing personality. Yet, to someone with social anxiety it meant the world. This was my introduction to the French Bistro.

The French Bistro was going to lessen the arguments I was going to have with my mother. This meant that my anxiety about being at the library was going to decrease as well. I was starting to create a schedule for where and when my beautiful angels were working. I started to spend most of my days at the French Bistro and most of my evenings at the library. The library was still too powerful a location of inspiration for me to lose because my beautiful blonde library angel was still working there. However, the French Bistro was giving some new life to my spiritual journey because of all the angels that were eating and working there. Plus, the French Bistro had healthier food for me to eat and I went their top get some unsweetened tea.

This did not mean that I was not drinking Pepsi while at the French Bistro. I was still getting my Pepsi from the nearby gas station before I went to the French Bistro. However, I was not buying my Pepsi at the French Bistro or getting refills there. I was going to the gas station because there was this beautiful angel that was working there. This beautiful angel was a very special angel because I was occasionally able to socialize with her when I got my soda from her. These social experiences I had with her were too important to lose. So, my routine was to go to this gas station every day to talk to the beautiful angel. Then, I went to the French Bistro to spend some time obsessing over the beautiful angels who were there before I went to the library.

My refusal to buy soda or get soda at the French Bistro led me to start drinking more unsweetened tea. This was helping me to feel healthier and eventually it led me to start running. Plus, the more time I spent at the French Bistro the more I started eating their food because I started to get hungry while there. The only problem with this routine was that it was an expensive routine. Yet, I felt the benefits to eating there outweighed the detriments to eating their because their food was both healthy and tasty. So, I felt their prices were worth it. However, the angels who were eating and working there were my main reason for going there.

These were all the reasons why the French Bistro turned into my new location of inspiration. These were all great reasons for me to return to the French Bistro. However, there was no better reason than the beautiful angel who introduced me to the French Bistro. This beautiful angel from the French Bistro was only a part of my journey for a short time. However, as my best friend once told me "It is about the quality of time, not the quantity of time. This statement definitely applies to the beautiful black haired angel from the French Bistro. The beautiful black haired angel from the French Bistro was only going to be there for two months.

This beautiful new angel from the French Bistro was very special. She was so special because she was so socially assertive and friendly. However, her introducing me to the concept of transference was really what made her special. I discovered how great the concept of transference was when my beautiful angel from the French Bistro left after her short time there. When she first left, I was saddened by her loss because she was so beautiful and friendly. However, this sadness did not last because I soon discovered that there was a beautiful blonde angel there to take her place. Then, I discovered that there were several other angels to obsess over after she left as well. I still had the beautiful blonde library angel to go to for inspiration. I had the beautiful blonde who replaced the beautiful angel who introduced me to the French Bistro. There was this beautiful red head that started working at the library. There was also this beautiful ebony angel who started working at the nearby library. Finally, there was this tall beautiful blonde angel who was working at the French Bistro. There was also this tall beautiful blonde manager who worked at the French Bistro. Oh, and I do not want to forget the only beautiful angel that I was socializing with at the nearby gas station. The point that I am trying to make is that there were many angels to take her place once she left. So, I am grateful to this beautiful angel for leaving because once she left, she introduced me to the power of transference.

Introducing me to all the beautiful angels that were out there was going to be a great discovery. This was such a powerful discovery because it was going to lead me to the realization that I could feel this spiritual energy with any beautiful woman. Although, I was not able to fully realize this variety until the beautiful angel from the French Bistro left for good. So, I believe another part of what made her so special was that she was only present for a short time. Once she disappeared, I was finally able to see the true power of transference. My obsession with beautiful women was not only going to be limited to my beautiful blonde library angel anymore.

This beautiful angel from the French Bistro was only there for a short time. She only worked at the French Bistro for about two months.

However, her impact continues to be felt to this day. I still feel her spiritual energy with all the beautiful angels that exist to obsess over. These beautiful women could be found anywhere and at different times. They could have any color hair. They could be of any ethnicity. They could be of any nationality. Finally, they could be of any age. Although, I usually find I am more attracted to women who are my age are younger. Yet, beauty is within the eye of the beholder and I believe there are men who are also attracted to older women. I am grateful that I am not attracted to older women though because this allows me to feel comfortable enough to socialize with them at times. However, there are times when it is difficult for me to talk to them as well. My attraction to beautiful women is usually the topic of discussion and this may make them annoyed and uncomfortable. So, let me take this opportunity to apologize to them now if this is the case. A moment never goes by when I am not thinking about a beautiful woman. These thoughts will consume 95% of all my thoughts. Yet, these same thoughts are also my source of inspiration for my passion for writing.

My learning to not be ashamed of my love for beautiful women and all my obsessions with beautiful women was very important to my passion for writing. This was important because it was such a powerful source of strength and inspiration. However, it was not going to be my only source of strength and inspiration. I was also going to find strength and inspiration from my passion for writing. I was finding that the cold was also important since I could not write if it was warm or hot. Then, there was my love for Pepsi. Sometimes I was able to drink unsweetened tea. Unfortunately, my love for the sweet taste of Pepsi was always too powerful.

My passion for music was the most powerful source of strength and inspiration. My passion for music was the most powerful because it was how I blocked out the rest of humanity. So, of all my sources of strength and inspiration this is the one that I could never live without because it is where I find my true passion. It is even greater than my love for beautiful women.

This book started out as a story about my beautiful blonde library angel. It started as a story about my obsession with this beautiful blonde librarian. However, as I continued to write my story it turned into a story about me celebrating the variety of beautiful women that existed. I celebrate their beauty because of my social anxiety. My social anxiety has me accepting the fact that I may never be able to verbally express my love for their beauty. My acceptance has me believing that I am invisible to beautiful women. This is not a life that I want to live, yet my inability to socialize has me believing that this is my reality. Although, my spiritual journey was starting to help me see things differently. I stopped being sad and depressed about my obsession with beautiful women, and instead I saw my obsessions with them as a source of strength. It all started with my beautiful blonde library angel who inspired me to start journaling. Eventually, journaling led me to my passion for writing which then gave birth to my spiritual journey. Finally, my spiritual journey introduced me to my passion for writing and to my beautiful angels.

Saying Goodbye

Saying goodbye to my beautiful blonde library angel was a day I was always going to dread. I was always going to dread this day because I knew that this meant the loss of the most important person to my life. Sure, I knew that there were going to be other beautiful angels to take her place once she left the library. Yet, the problem I always had with all these other beautiful angels after she left the library was that none of these other beautiful angels were her.

My spiritual journey with my beautiful blonde library angel was the most powerful journey of my life because it introduced me to my passion for writing. My passion for writing was important because it presented me with a safe outlet to express myself. I needed a safe outlet for expressing myself since I could not verbally express myself due to my social anxiety. When I was around people, my mind went blank. There were some days I could go the entire day without saying a word to anyone. Yet, as bad as this social anxiety was, this was not the only reason why I was not able to verbally express myself. Another reason why I found it difficult to express myself verbally was because I was always thinking about beautiful women.

Most of my thoughts during my spiritual journey were about beautiful women. I was constantly thinking about where and when

I might be able to see one of these beautiful angels. I had about ten beautiful angels I was planning my day around as I started to write this chapter. The beautiful blonde library angel was still one of the beautiful angels that I was obsessed over. There were the three beautiful angels who were taking her place when she was not working at the library. The beautiful creative library angel was still working at the library when I was writing this chapter. Then, there were these two new library angels who started working at the library as the other library angels were being phased out of the library. One of these beautiful new library angels was this beautiful ebony girl who started working there. However, it was not right away that I found her attractive. It was not right away that I found her attractive because she was always trying to hide her beauty with comic book T-shirts and messy hair. I could tell she was attractive though, since she had a great body and a beautiful face. This beautiful ebony angel was not the only new library angel that I was obsessing over at the library.

There was one other beautiful angel who worked at the library that I found attractive. This last angel was as beautiful as the beautiful blonde library angel. This was part of the reason why I was never really that attracted to the ebony angel. I found that her beauty was always overshadowed by the beauty of this new red headed angel and my beautiful blonde library angel.

This new red headed angel started working at the library around the same time as the ebony angel. This fiery red head was going to be an important part of my second book because I thought she was going to carry the torch for my beautiful blonde library angel once she left. I thought this because she was walking though the library talking to her when I first saw her. This was my introduction to the red headed angel that I started to call my fiery red head. I honestly believed she was going to carry the torch for my beautiful blonde library angel when she left. The more I believed that she was being passed the torch, the more I felt the magic of the library with this fiery red head. Unfortunately, I was going to later learn that she was not my new library angel because she left the library the day after my beautiful blonde library angel also left.

There were four beautiful library angels left at the library as I was completing the last chapter of *The Beautiful Blonde Library Angel*. I was still going to the library to see the library angels that were left. Then, I was going to the French Bistro to see all the beautiful angels working there, and there was still the beautiful angel that was working at the gas station. The beautiful angel working at the gas station continued to be a very special angel. She still continued to be this special angel because she was someone, I was able to socialize with at times.

These were only brief conversations that lasted about a minute or two. They could sometimes last about five minutes if I was feeling really confident. Though these were only brief conversations, they meant a great deal to my confidence at the time. These brief conversations with her were helping me to contradict my belief that I could not talk to beautiful women. Sure, I still felt anxious around her and I knew I had no chance with her since she had a boyfriend. I knew she had a boyfriend because she mentioned it quite a bit during our brief conversations. However, I still continued to go to the gas station for these brief conversations with her since I knew I had to start somewhere. Then, after I had these brief conversations with her, I was spending several hours at the French Bistro before returning to the gas station to see her again.

I spent most of my days and nights at the French Bistro once it turned into my new location of inspiration. I knew my beautiful angels from the library were only at the library from four to eight certain weekdays, and for four hours Saturdays. So, my time at the library was always limited. Then, I was only at the gas station for about five minutes to talk to this beautiful angel from the gas station as I went there for my Pepsi. The rest of my time I was at the French Bistro to see the beautiful angels working there. There was this tall beautiful blonde angel who was working there that I found very attractive. Sadly, as attractive as she was, I never did find her very inspirational until she said hi to me about a year later when I was going to see who was at Control one night. Then, there was this dark-skinned brunette angel who was somewhat attractive, however I hated her personality since I felt she was more annoyed by me being there. Finally, there was a beautiful blonde angel who was going to be an important angel to my spiritual journey after my beautiful blonde library angel left the library finally about a year ago.

My obsessions with my beautiful angels were all I was thinking about and I loved it because they were inspiring me to write my book. They were inspiring me to live my life again. They were inspiring me since they were my writing muses. The only problem I had with my obsessions with beautiful women was that they were not helping me deal with my social anxiety.

I did not believe anyone could ever possibly understand my thoughts about beautiful women. I did not believe anyone could understand how I could spend so many years obsessing over beautiful women at my locations of inspiration. I did not believe anyone could understand how I could be around so many beautiful women and never say anything to them. So, ultimately, I did not believe anyone could understand my debilitating social anxiety. So, I never spoke to anyone about my social anxiety because 95 % of all my thoughts were about beautiful women.

Yet, these same thoughts were what made my life worth living. So, as bothersome as these thoughts were because they were making it difficult for me to socialize, I refused to let them go.

These thoughts were consuming me, and I needed a safe outlet to express myself. My beautiful blonde library angel gave me this safe outlet by leading me to my passion for writing. I could not find enough time to write about beautiful women once I found this safe outlet. I could not find enough time since there were so many angels inspiring my journey. I started my spiritual journey with only my beautiful blonde library angel. I had now found over ten angels.

My spiritual journey with these beautiful angels started the moment I discovered my beautiful blonde library angel at the library. I lost my beautiful blonde library angel over a year ago when she finally left the library forever. The French Bistro near Bon Gout was my new location of inspiration once she left the library to never return. However, the beautiful angel that kept me at the French Bistro changed after she left. The beautiful angel that kept me there was not the beautiful black haired angel with glasses since she was also gone. Instead, the angel who was keeping me there was this blonde angel I previously mentioned who was now a supervisor.

This French Bistro near Bon Gout was my only location of inspiration for quite some time after my beautiful blonde library angel left. This was what made this beautiful blonde at my original Bon Gout such a special angel at the time. She was the only beautiful angel that I had left after my beautiful blonde library angel left because the angel from the gas station also left. Thus, for about a month or two all I had was the beautiful blonde supervisor working at Bon Gout. Then, I started going to another French Bistro that I discovered when I started to work at this call center. This new French Bistro was a great addition to my spiritual journey because there were so many beautiful angels that were both working and eating there. I even found myself socializing with some of these beautiful angels as I kept going there to write. Sadly, nothing happened with them after this since they did not remain at my new French Bistro. However, this French Bistro remained an important part of my spiritual journey after they left.

The discovery of my new French Bistro had me seeing my two locations of inspiration differently. I started to think of my original French Bistro as the safe and comfortable location of inspiration. Then, I thought of my new French Bistro as the one where I was more anxious at because I thought I might have a chance with some of these angels. However, the more time that I spent at my new French Bistro, the more comfortable I felt there as well. I was starting to feel more comfortable there because of how welcoming these angels were there. I was especially feeling more confident there because of the inspiration I felt from the supervisors working there.

The two supervisors that were helping me feel more confident were both very attractive and they each had different personalities. One was this beautiful red head who was reserved and quiet. The other was a beautiful black haired angel who later dyed her hair blonde which made her even more special since I started to imagine she did this because she read my book. This black haired angel was very outgoing and friendly. So, these two supervisors were literally total opposites. This made it difficult for me to single one out as the woman of my dreams. My spiritual journey with these two supervisors followed a different a path as well. When I started going to my new French Bistro, I never thought I might have a chance with the outgoing one. However, I thought maybe I might have a chance with the quiet one. Then, the quiet one sat facing me only a booth away from me and I thought this was a sign of interest.

Once I thought I might have a chance with her, I thought I might have a chance with other women there as well. I even started to approach some of the beautiful angels who went there to study and eat. Finally, about a year or so later, I started to imagine having a chance with the outgoing supervisor. Today, I feel both of these supervisors are equally important to my spiritual journey. I believe that either one of them could be the woman of my dreams. However, I find that the more confident I get, the more I think that the more outgoing angel could be the woman of my dreams.

The Coronavirus Pandemic caused me to temporarily lose both French Bistros as my locations of inspiration. I was still able to go there to get an unsweetened tea and to see which of the beautiful angels were working there before work. However, getting my unsweetened tea only took about five minutes and then I had to leave. I could not go there for my writing since the dining area was closed. So, my French Bistros were only my locations of inspiration for a few minutes as the Coronavirus first hit. Then, I went to a department store nearby while I was waiting to go home. The name of this department store was called Control. Walking into Control was a great idea, because I saw that there were so many beautiful angels working there.

The first angel I saw when I walked into Control was this beautiful blonde who I was calling the beautiful purplish blonde angel because she had purple dye within her hair Then, I saw this blonde angel stocking the beauty area and I started to call her the angel of beauty. Eventually, I also saw this blonde angel at the front of the store by the carts and I called her the beautiful blonde cart angel. There was a beautiful blonde security guard and also this black angel who I called my black beauty. There were these two beautiful, tanned brunettes that could have been twins since I thought of them as being the same women until I saw their name tags. There was also a beautiful blonde supervisor and a beautiful black-haired angel. These ten beautiful angels had introduced me to Control as a new location of inspiration during the virus.

I spent four years writing and rewriting *The Beautiful Blonde Library Angel* at my locations of inspiration. My first location of inspiration was the library. I lost the library as my location of inspiration when my beautiful blonde library angel left. However, I never lost her spiritual presence since her spiritual presence will always be felt within my passion for writing.

The story of my first book has been all about introducing my beautiful blonde library angel and my spiritual journey with her. I first realized the story of my first book after spending three days mourning over her supposed loss. I say supposed loss because she returned to the library after these three days of mourning. My three days of mourning started Thursday May 24th, 2018 and lasted until Saturday May 26th, 2018. My three days of mourning started with me sitting at the library thinking that she had quit since two weeks passed since I last saw her. After two weeks of not seeing her at the library, I realized this might be it and I might never see her again. This led me into a devastating state of depression that started with me sitting at the library looking out the window at the library. As I thought about her not being at the library anymore, I could not feel the magic there anymore. So, I decided to write at the French Bistro.

I spent the rest of my time mourning over her supposed loss at the French Bistro. I was spending my time there writing about the impact that she had upon my life. Before I could write about her impact though I felt the need to write about some of my other major losses. I wrote about the loss of my "My Wonderful French Childhood". I wrote about how I had lost all hope of ever being with a beautiful woman. I wrote about the loss of my friends from high school when I moved to Ohio. I wrote about the loss of trying to live a normal life because of my social anxiety and my age. My writing about all of these losses eventually had me writing about the supposed loss of my beautiful blonde library angel and why she was so important to my journey.

I realized what the story of my first book was going to be about as I was looking out the window of my original French Bistro. I spent three days mourning over the supposed loss of my beautiful blonde library angel from the library. Then, I thought about what I was really losing with her being gone. I was thinking about how I was never going to see her physical beauty at the library again. I was thinking how I was never going to hear her giggle as she laughed again. I was thinking how I was never going to see her smile again. I was thinking how I was never going to see how she enjoyed joking around and talking to the other library angels again. All of these things were the things I was going to miss if she left the library. I was devastated by the idea of never seeing her again. Then, as I spent these three days writing about what I was losing by never seeing her physical presence at the library again, I started to celebrate her presence. I started celebrating all that I might never have discovered if she never appeared into my life at all.

I started to celebrate the spiritual journey she gave birth to by appearing into my life when she did. I started to celebrate how her beauty led me out of my pit of darkness. I started to celebrate how her beauty was keeping me at the library so that I could discover my passion for writing. Finally, I celebrated the spiritual energy my angels possessed even if I never said a word to them.

I feared I might lose my passion for writing when she stopped working at the library. The greatest fear I had was that if she stopped working at the library my inspiration might leave with her. Luckily, this never happened when she left because during her supposed loss, I was able to find inspiration elsewhere. I was able to find inspiration from the other beautiful library angels who were still working at the library. I was able to find inspiration from the beautiful angels who were eating and working at the French Bistro. I was able to find inspiration from my passion for writing without her presence. I found my inspiration from the cold and from my Pepsi. Finally, my greatest source of inspiration was going to derive from my passion for music.

My passion for music was my greatest source of strength and inspiration during my spiritual journey with her. Today, anytime that I hear two albums I am reminded of my spiritual journey with my beautiful blonde library angel. The first album that reminds me of my spiritual journey with her is Mana's "Drama Y Luz" because of this album's one song. "Vuela Libre Paloma" was a very powerful song since it was the theme song to my spiritual journey with her. I do not speak Spanish. Yet, every time that I hear this song, I understand each and every word. The most inspirational and spiritual line from this song is "You are my lighthouse in the storm that illuminates my darkness". It continues with "You are my guardian angel, and in the sky, my love…I will find you." This inspirational and spiritual song by Mana takes me to another spiritual plane every time I hear it because I imagine it being about my spiritual journey with her.

The second album to remind me of my spiritual journey with her is a French album by Vianney. This French album by Vianney reminds me of our spiritual journey together since this French album was the album that set the mood for my time of mourning. I have no clue how many times I listened to this album over the course of my three days of mourning. All I know is that I never wanted to stop listening to it since it was healing me from her supposed loss. It was during this time of mourning that I discovered the power of my passion for music. My passion for music inspired me to write twenty-five pages about her. I wrote about her loss and why she meant so much to my life. Throughout my two-year spiritual journey with her, I was always thinking that my beautiful blonde library angel was my greatest source of strength. Then, during her supposed loss, I discovered that my passion for music was also a source of strength. I even sometimes feel as if my passion for music is more powerful than my love for beautiful women. I believe this because of how I feel when I listen to music. There is nothing like the power of a good song or album and I felt this with Mana and Vianney. I always thought that if I was shipwrecked and I could have only one thing, then this one thing has to be my passion for music.

How was I going to say goodbye to my beautiful blonde library angel? How could I say goodbye to the spark that gave birth to my spiritual journey with my passion for writing? These were two very good questions that I could not answer. I started thinking the best way for me to say goodbye to her was to say goodbye to her at a time when I had some control over seeing her. So, when I found out she had not left the library after her supposed loss, I started spending more time at the French Bistro. I spent more time there to phase her out of my life when she left the library for good. This was what made my two French Bistros such an important part of my life.

It has now been four years since I first started my spiritual journey with my beautiful blonde library angel. It has been over a year now since the beautiful blonde library angel and the magic of the library stopped being a part of my spiritual journey. I do not know where my spiritual journey will lead me now. I do not know if it will lead me to the woman of my dreams or not. I hope it leads me to her, yet I do not know if it will or not. I also do not know who the woman of my dreams might be if she does exist. She could be this beautiful angel with black hair that I am obsessing over as I am writing the last page of my book. However, I do not know if this is her or not. So, as I close the last chapter of my book, the woman of my dreams still remains a mystery. However, what does not remain a mystery is how my spiritual journey of trying to discover her all started four years ago. I will never allow myself to forget that my spiritual journey all started with me getting my first glimpse of the beautiful blonde library angel.

Made in the USA
Middletown, DE
01 September 2024